A Christmas Keepsake from the Irish Hermitage

A Christmas Keepsake from the Irish Hermitage

Proceeds from this book go to feed the hungry and clothe the naked. We thank you for your purchase.

To see some of our other products, go to www.xanga.com/sistersofgraceofchrist

ISBN: 978-0-9809317-3-0

A Christmas Keepsake
from
the Irish Hermitage

by a Nun of Grace

Contents

Introduction...

Nestling into the green-shawled breast on an Irish mountain a small hermitage hides...

Reached only by a bridge, it is girded on the other three sides by water... two fast-flowing streams and the wide, restless sea...

Trees shelter it lovingly... old native ash and alder, rowan and willow; hawthorn and fuchsia hedge it...

Here dwells a Nun, a Monastic Solitary, living apart from her Order in a work of cloistered Prayer.

Sister wears the full, traditional Monastic Habit of her Order. Full-length, black habit, deep blue scapular, white guimp and large white wimple, and her veil is long, deep blue lined with white.

In these modest garments, she is known and visibly a Nun.

The skills of her hands in her seclusion support the care of the homeless, especially children, in many lands where her Sisters in Christ Jesus live out their calling among the most needy of mankind...

Her outgoings are few, for essentials only, her visitors fewer. Her love for others expressed in her separation...

Hers are the seasons, the flowers and food she tends in her gardens... the wild flowers... Hers the first birdsong of the day, the last sweet vespers they linger in…

Hers too are the creatures who enrich her life… Those no one wants, like the little ones her Sisters care for… the lost, the sick, the crippled…

These reflections and stories and poems are single threads in a tapestry woven and stitched over many years.

Single blossoms in a bouquet… gleanings and gatherings along the quiet lanes of the years.

And this, the Christmas season, rich in tradition.

Above and in all they reflect the heart-life of a Monastic Nun, to whom everything becomes prayer.

I hold in my hands a star
Its vibrant light lifting it from palms
Which curve to cherish it.

I keep in my heart a joy,
A pause of eternity –
Caught from the silent hours.

My hands and my heart are vessels
Weak and frail as the tiniest shell
Caught in the swell of endless tides..
Launched against shores of jagged rocks
Helpless in the rhythm of the earth

My hands must hold other things,
Move from their curve of prayer
To other things.

Yet He is there
In my hands and heart,
The miracle...

And He will not move though I move.

Prologue…

The wildening wind, heavy with icy rain, all but blew Sister in through the porch door.

She dropped the sodden creel of dripping greenery on the tiles.

The storm, great black clouds rolling in off the ocean, had struck suddenly when she was at the far end of the grounds, reaching up with the walking stick handle to crook down a magnificent branch of scarlet-berried holly.

Heavy and hard the rain blew at her all the way back, buffeting and bullying.

But the creel was well-filled…enough for the Advent Wreath, and garlands for door and gate.

Pine branches, resinous and fragrant, and most of all, holly and ivy..

As Sister shed her wet boots and dripping cape, she sang softly that old carol, the wild wind howling and keening, the rain drumming and fretting.

So full of the ancient symbolism and deep meaning; investing everything with the abiding faith in Jesus…

The holly and the ivy,
When they are both full grown,
Of all the trees that are in the wood,
The holly bears the crown.

The holly bears a blossom
As white as lily flower,
And Mary bore sweet Jesus Christ,
To be our sweet saviour.

The holly bears a berry
As red as any blood,
And Mary bore sweet Jesus Christ,
To do poor sinners good.

The holly bears a prickle,
As sharp as any thorn,
And Mary bore sweet Jesus Christ,
On Christmas Day in the morn.

The holly bears a bark,
As bitter as any gall,
And Mary bore sweet Jesus Christ,
For to redeem us all.

Strong, simple truths.

Sister was pensive as she went through to the main room, barefoot, and sought dry socks and slippers.

She had been too long away, and the fire was almost out, the room quickly cooling as the temperature dropped sharply.

The cats were huddled together on her chair, eyes wide and reproachful.

"Poor waifs," she chuckled, caressing smooth heads.

If the wind dropped, there would be frost, she thought, as she rebuilt the fire with wood and turf atop firelighters.

Watching the small flames flicker and grow, blossoming their fragrant warmth into the room.

Almost dark already; so she hurried out again to do the last chores of feeding and bringing in turf against the night chill.

A long evening ahead, and still the words of the ancient carol throbbed through her soul, spilling out in soft humming.

Advent here almost, and the wreath to make…

She made her simple supper, and sat a while, pensive, the two cats at her feet, curled intertwined on the rug as they loved to be, as they had been since the womb.

Content now in the warmth.

Holding in her fingers a small sprig of holly... three leaves and three bright berries.

The entirety of faith encapsulated in one small spray.

She fingered it softly, then lifted her fingers to her mouth, tasting the bitterness of the bark as she gazed at the berries, gentling the sharp points of the leaves, lost in reverie and prayer.

All the beauty and all the pain endured. The love given so freely and fully.

And yet how few realised the meaning, the reason for the holly…

Or the true and only reason for the season, simply.

The room warmed and glowed with the firelight.

And her heart turned to the Christmas she and her Sisters knew.

The Christmas that was simple and gentle; yet that gave to others also.

That dual thread that ran through their lives; of giving and loving.

That ran through the lives of so many who knew and loved the Lord Jesus.

How to express and live that in a world where so many were in desperate need; and so many in more spiritual need than they knew, surrounded by more than they knew what to do with.

To find the balance that was of Jesus.

Not a killjoy; but not profligate and meaningless.

Once more, she turned to old files and papers, scattering sheets and scraps over the table and her lap.

Seeking ways and words to tell this; the great beauty and comfort, yet the giving that was the greatest beauty and comfort.

And as she pored over words and books, she saw that so many others had ached as she did now, to put into words what was inexpressible.

She glimpsed depths and realities she had never known before in all that she read.

People in their own situations and life settings, striving to live the love of Jesus in whatever ways they had.

The giving, the caring, in simple ways.

Always behind the seemingly trivial, the emotions.

For the gift of giving is in the love of it, not the size or quality of it.

As Jesus taught of the widow's mite... For she gave not of her excess but of her very substance.

And the poorest in the world's eyes, thus could and did give more than a millionaire.

Not the tinsel, hoarded carefully year after year, but the loving hands that draped it.

Giving it grace and beauty.

Not a tawdry ornament, but the love and thought that had chosen it so painstakingly.

Like the teenage girl she had noticed in the pound shop, agonising over which gift pack of bath cubes and soap to buy her mother.

Her forehead wrinkled, her eyes dark.

Sister had smiled and said, "She will love whichever you give, because you chose it."

And seen the young face relax and smile.

And so the garnering and ordering began.

There was one carol that seemed to encapsulate so much and so simply…

So she started to divide all that she had read into its parts, verse by verse.

A work that was to absorb her all through Advent – her own preparation in the Silence and Solitude that were her welcome lot, for Christmas.

And that night, Sister laid the sprig of holly, the three glossy leaves where the three bright berries nestle, on the Prayer Table in her small oratory under the star, to remind her always of these things…

The First Verse

In the bleak midwinter,
Frosty wind made moan,
Earth stood hard as iron,
Water like a stone.
Snow had fallen,
Snow on snow,
Snow on snow…
In the bleak midwinter,
Long ago…

Before the Light...

Sister sat, rapt by firelight, watching the small flames flickering round the turf.

Feeling the welcome heat on her skin as she bent to sweep the hearth, gently working round the sleeping cats.

Who looked far too comfortable to move.

Warmth kindled in need, at will, easily.

And for many, simply the pressing of a switch. The roar of the central heating boiler and the ticking of the radiators as they filled with heat.

Sister pondered… the huge need of the poor. For the simple basic human needs, that thankfully so many are able to take almost for granted.

Those who last year, last Christmas, had a home, a bed, who celebrated Christmas in warmth and family. Light and heat and good food.

Who this year, through no fault of theirs, slept cold on city streets.

The desolation of the poor and hungry.

And the stories that spoke of this. Of the utter needs.

Where human love abandoned humans.

And Sister thought too of the coldness of "charity": the condescension...

Of giving not given for love…

And two of the papers scattered before her spoke of these things.

The Little Match Girl

by Hans Christian Andersen

Most terribly cold it was; it snowed, and was nearly quite dark, and evening - the last evening of the year.

In this cold and darkness there went along the street a poor little girl, bareheaded, and with naked feet.

When she left home she had slippers on, it is true; but what was the good of that? They were very large slippers, which her mother had hitherto worn; so large were they; and the poor little thing lost them as she scuffled away across the street, because of two carriages that rolled by dreadfully fast.

One slipper was nowhere to be found; the other had been laid hold of by an urchin, and off he ran with it; he thought it would do capitally for a cradle when he some day or other should have children himself.

So the little maiden walked on with her tiny naked feet, that were quite red and blue from cold.

She carried a quantity of matches in an old apron, and she held a bundle of them in her hand. Nobody had bought anything of her the whole livelong day; no one had given her a single farthing.

She crept along trembling with cold and hunger - a very picture of sorrow, the poor little thing!

The flakes of snow covered her long fair hair, which fell in beautiful curls around her neck; but of that, of course, she never once now thought.

From all the windows the candles were gleaming, and it smelt so deliciously of roast goose, for you know it was New Year's Eve; yes, of that she thought.

In a corner formed by two houses, of which one advanced more than the other, she seated herself down and cowered together.

Her little feet she had drawn close up to her, but she grew colder and colder, and to go home she did not venture, for she had not sold any matches and could not bring a farthing of money: from her father she would certainly get blows, and at home it was cold too, for above her she had only the roof, through which the wind whistled, even though the largest cracks were stopped up with straw and rags.

Her little hands were almost numbed with cold. Oh! A match might afford her a world of comfort, if she only dared take a single one out of the bundle, draw it against the wall, and warm her fingers by it.

She drew one out. "Rischt!" How it blazed, how it burnt! It was a warm, bright flame, like a candle, as she held her hands over it: it was a wonderful light. It seemed really to the little maiden as though she were sitting before a large iron stove, with burnished brass feet and a brass ornament at top. The fire burned with such blessed influence; it warmed so delightfully.

The little girl had already stretched out her feet to warm them too; but—the small flame went out, the stove vanished: she had only the remains of the burnt-out match in her hand.

She rubbed another against the wall: it burned brightly, and where the light fell on the wall, there the wall became transparent like a veil, so that she could see into the room. On the table was spread a snow-white tablecloth; upon it was a splendid porcelain service, and the roast goose was steaming famously with its stuffing of apple and dried plums.

And what was still more capital to behold was, the goose hopped down from the dish, reeled about on the floor with knife and fork in its breast, till it came up to the poor little girl; when - the match went out and nothing but the thick, cold, damp wall was left behind.

She lighted another match. Now there she was sitting under the most magnificent Christmas tree: it was still larger, and more decorated than the one which she had seen through the glass door in the rich merchant's house.

Thousands of lights were burning on the green branches, and gaily-colored pictures, such as she had seen in the shop-windows, looked down upon her. The little maiden stretched out her hands towards them when—the match went out. The lights of the Christmas tree rose higher and higher, she saw them now as stars in heaven; one fell down and formed a long trail of fire.

"Someone is just dead!" said the little girl; for her old grandmother, the only person who had loved her, and who was now no more, had told her, that when a star falls, a soul ascends to God.

She drew another match against the wall: it was again light, and in the lustre there stood the old grandmother, so bright and radiant, so mild, and with such an expression of love.

"Grandmother!" cried the little one. "Oh, take me with you! You go away when the match burns out; you vanish like the warm stove, like the delicious roast goose, and like the magnificent Christmas tree!"

And she rubbed the whole bundle of matches quickly against the wall, for she wanted to be quite sure of keeping her grandmother near her.

And the matches gave such a brilliant light that it was brighter than at noon-day: never formerly had the grandmother been so beautiful and so tall. She took the little maiden, on her arm, and both flew in brightness and in joy so high, so very high, and then above was neither cold, nor hunger, nor anxiety—they were with God.

But in the corner, at the cold hour of dawn, sat the poor girl, with rosy cheeks and with a smiling mouth, leaning against the wall—frozen to death on the last evening of the old year.

Stiff and stark sat the child there with her matches, of which one bundle had been burnt. "She wanted to warm herself," people said.

No one had the slightest suspicion of what beautiful things she had seen; no one even dreamed of the splendor in which, with her grandmother she had entered on the joys of a new year.

Christmas Day in the Workhouse
George R. Sims (1903)

It is Christmas Day in the workhouse,
And the cold, bare walls are bright
With garlands of green and holly,
And the place is a pleasant sight;
For with clean-washed hands and
faces,
In a long and hungry line
The paupers sit at the table,
For this is the hour they dine.

And the guardians and their ladies,
Although the wind is east,
Have come in their furs and wrappers,
To watch their charges feast;
To smile and be condescending,
Put pudding on pauper plates.
To be hosts at the workhouse banquet
They've paid for — with the rates.

Oh, the paupers are meek and lowly
With their 'Thank'ee kindly, mum's';
So long as they fill their stomachs,
What matter it whence it comes!
But one of the old men mutters,
And pushes his plate aside:
"Great God!" he cries, "but it chokes me!
For this is the day she died!"

The guardians gazed in horror,
The master's face went white;
"Did a pauper refuse the pudding?"
"Could their ears believe aright?"
Then the ladies clutched their husbands,
Thinking the man would die,
Struck by a bolt, or something,
By the outraged One on high.

But the pauper sat for a moment,
Then rose 'mid silence grim,
For the others had ceased to chatter
And trembled in every limb.
He looked at the guardians' ladies,
Then, eyeing their lords, he said,
"I eat not the food of villains
Whose hands are foul and red:

"Whose victims cry for vengeance
From their dark, unhallowed graves."
"He's drunk!" said the workhouse master,
"Or else he's mad and raves."
"Not drunk or mad," cried the pauper,
"But only a haunted beast,
Who, torn by the hounds and mangled,
Declines the vulture's feast.

"I care not a curse for the guardians,
And I won't be dragged away;
Just let me have the fit out,
It's only on Christmas Day
That the black past comes to goad me,
And prey on my burning brain;
I'll tell you the rest in a whisper —
I swear I won't shout again.

"Keep your hands off me, curse you!
Hear me right out to the end.
You come here to see how paupers
The season of Christmas spend;.
You come here to watch us feeding,
As they watched the captured beast.
Here's why a penniless pauper
Spits on your paltry feast.

"Do you think I will take your bounty,
And let you smile and think
You're doing a noble action
With the parish's meat and drink?
Where is my wife, you traitors —
The poor old wife you slew?
Yes, by the God above me,
My Nance was killed by you!

"Last winter my wife lay dying,
Starved in a filthy den;
I had never been to the parish—
I came to the parish then.
I swallowed my pride in coming,
For ere the ruin came,
I held up my head as a trader,
And I bore a spotless name.

"I came to the parish, craving
Bread for a starving wife,
Bread for the woman who'd loved me
Through fifty years of life;
And what do you think they told me,
Mocking my awful grief,
That 'the House' was open to us,
But they wouldn't give 'out relief'.

"I slunk to the filthy alley—
'Twas a cold, raw Christmas Eve—
And the bakers' shops were open,
Tempting a man to thieve;
But I clenched my fists together,
Holding my head awry,
So I came to her empty-handed
And mournfully told her why.

"Then I told her the house was open;
She had heard of the ways of that,
For her bloodless cheeks went crimson,
and up in her rags she sat,
Crying, 'Bide the Christmas here, John,
We've never had one apart;
I think I can bear the hunger—
The other would break my heart.'

"All through that eve I watched her,
Holding her hand in mine,
Praying the Lord and weeping,
Till my lips were salt as brine;
I asked her once if she hungered,
And as she answered 'No',
The moon shone in at the window,
Set in a wreath of snow.

"Then the room was bathed in glory,
And I saw in my darling's eyes
The faraway look of wonder
That comes when the spirit flies;
And her lips were parched and parted,
And her reason came and went.
For she raved of our home in Devon,
Where our happiest years were spent.

"And the accents, long forgotten,
Came back to the tongue once more.
For she talked like the country lassie
I woo'd by the Devon shore;
Then she rose to her feet and trembled,
And fell on the rags and moaned,
And, 'Give me a crust--I'm famished--
For the love of God!' she groaned.

"I rushed from the room like a madman
And flew to the workhouse gate,
Crying, 'Food for a dying woman!'
And the answer came, 'Too late.'
They drove me away with curses;
Then I fought with a dog in the street
And tore from the mongrel's clutches
A crust he was trying to eat.

"Back through the filthy byways!
Back through the trampled slush!
Up to the crazy garret,
Wrapped in an awful hush;
My heart sank down at the threshold,
And I paused with a sudden thrill.
For there, in the silv'ry moonlight,
My Nance lay, cold and still.

"Up to the blackened ceiling,
The sunken eyes were cast—
I knew on those lips, all bloodless,
My name had been the last;
She called for her absent husband—
O God! had I but known!—
Had called in vain, and, in anguish,
Had died in that den—alone.

"Yes, there, in a land of plenty,
Lay a loving woman dead,
Cruelly starved and murdered
for a loaf of the parish bread;
At yonder gate, last Christmas,
I craved for a human life,
You, who would feed us paupers,
What of my murdered wife!"

"There, get ye gone to your dinners,
Don't mind me in the least,
Think of the happy paupers
Eating your Christmas feast;
And when you recount their blessings
In your smug parochial way,
Say what you did for me, too,
Only last Christmas Day."

Cold, cold, cold as ice. Not the warmth and lovingkindness of God in Jesus.

Icy as snow... Bound in bitter chill.

Not the love that gives and gives all, with no thought save of giving.

Sister shivered; the fire had again burned low. Like all living things, it needed feeding, and blessed she knew herself to have fuel and shelter, food and all things needful.

Both her entries were in times past, but they were as new and modern as the day dawning.

And the fire made no inroads to the chill in her heart as her thoughts reached out to those on the streets of this world, where there were not now workhouses.

And the shining awareness that when you give to others, then you give to Jesus, and so you give the best and the utmost that you have and are.

And an old, old rhyme drifted into her head, making her smile….

Always the courage, always the hope, always that defiance in the face of poverty.

Christmas is coming; the geese are getting fat.

Please to put a penny in the old man's hat.

If you haven't got a penny, a halfpenny will do,

If you haven't got a halfpenny?

GOD BLESS YOU!

The Second Verse...

Our God, heaven cannot hold Him,
Nor the earth sustain.
Heaven and earth shall flee away,
When He comes again.

In the bleak midwinter,
A stable place sufficed,
The Lord God Almighty, Jesus Christ.

Towards the Light...

Advent Sunday, and rain falling soft and straight.

Fire fuel heaped high in creels...

First candle lit...

Burning tall and true and bright among the greenery and ribbons.

Cats gazing at the fire, their fur too hot to touch.

All tidied for the early evening as the dim daylight faded softly.

And Sister's thoughts, gazing at the simply crafted wreath, turned to the old customs, the ancient ways of preparing for Christmas…

The wreath, round as the world.

And so many thoughts of what colour the candles were to be!

Sister smiled ruefully, remembering the year an email had arrived asking her to adjudicate in a "discussion" between two brothers in the same house. It had grown so heated that they had decided to do away with the wreath altogether.

Her response had been very simple... It is the Light that matters, not the colour of the candles.

So she had told them what she did. Her own choice was white... four tall candles, and a central larger white for the Christ, Light of the World.

It was so simple...

And so many old traditions and customs.

Beauty and riches.

The Jesse Tree!

Sister smiled as the computer screen lit up... Starlight, and the candles flickering and blazing strong and true, on the tall Christmas Tree...

And the gentle old carol, sweet and calm.

This was a favourite site, a wonder of the internet. Skill and technology creating truth and beauty.

Delighting the senses and strengthening the soul.

Old, old custom, of the Jesse Tree… the full wonder of the Messianic Prophecies.

Ah, but here they are only listed. Books and numbers, not the full text.

So Sister sat and carefully, lovingly, worn Bible in front of the computer, typed out just a few of the hundreds of texts.

Of the promises and prophecies given by God…

All the wondrous foreseeings, in such precise detail, hundreds of years before the Nativity.

Jesus, born in Bethlehem…

"But thou, Bethlehem Ephratah, though thou be little among the thousands of Judah, yet out of thee shall He come forth unto Me that is to be Ruler in Israel, whose goings forth have been from of old, from Everlasting." Micah 5:2

Jesus, born of a Virgin…

"Therefore the Lord himself shall give you a sign; Behold, a virgin shall conceive, and bear a Son, and shall call His name Immanuel." Isaiah 7:14

Jesus, Son of Man...

"I saw in the night visions, and, behold, one like the Son of Man came with the clouds of heaven, and came to the Ancient of Days, and they brought Him near before Him.

"And there was given Him dominion, and glory, and a kingdom, that all people, nations, and languages, should serve Him:

"His Dominion is an everlasting dominion, which shall not pass away, and His Kingdom that which shall not be destroyed." Daniel 7:13-14

Son of Jacob

"I shall see Him, but not now: I shall behold Him, but not nigh: there shall come a Star out of Jacob, and a Sceptre shall rise out of Israel." Numbers 24:17

Stem of Jesse

"And there shall come forth a rod out of the stem of Jesse, and a Branch shall grow out of his roots. And the spirit of the Lord shall rest upon him, the spirit of wisdom and understanding, the spirit of counsel and might, the spirit of knowledge and of the fear of the Lord. And shall make him of quick understanding in the fear of the Lord; and he shall not judge after the sight of his eyes, neither reprove after the hearing of his ears, but with righteousness shall he judge the poor, and reprove with equity for the meek of the earth. And he shall smite the earth with the rod of his mouth, and with the breath of his lips shall he slay the wicked. And righteousness shall be the girdle of his loins, and faithfulness the girdle of his reins. The wolf also shall dwell with the lamb, and the leopard shall lie down with the kid; and the calf and the young lion and the fatling together; and a little child shall lead them. And the cow and the bear shall feed; their young ones shall lie down together: and the lion shall eat straw like the ox. And the sucking child shall play on the hole of the asp, and the weaned child shall put his hand on the cockatrice' den. They shall not hurt nor destroy in all my holy mountain: for the earth shall be full of the knowledge of the Lord, as the waters cover the sea.

And in that day there shall be a root of Jesse, which shall stand for an ensign of the people; to it shall the Gentiles seek: and his rest shall be glorious." Isaiah 11; 1-12

Son of David:

"Behold, the days come, saith The Lord, that I will raise unto David a righteous Branch, and a King shall reign and prosper, and shall execute judgment and justice in the earth.

"In His days Judah shall be saved, and Israel shall dwell safely: and this is His Name whereby He shall be called, THE LORD OUR RIGHTEOUSNESS." Jeremiah 23:5-6

Jesus, The Good Shepherd:

"O Zion, that bringest good tidings, get thee up into the high mountain; O Jerusalem, that bringest good tidings, lift up thy voice with strength; lift it up, be not afraid; say unto the cities of Judah, Behold your God! Behold, the Lord God will come with strong hand, and his arm shall rule for him: behold, his reward is with him, and his work before him.

"He shall feed his flock like a shepherd: he shall gather the lambs with his arm, and carry them in his bosom, and shall gently lead those that are with young." Isaiah 40:9-11

Jesus, riding into Jerusalem, on a Donkey:

"Rejoice greatly, O daughter of Zion; shout, O daughter of Jerusalem: behold, thy King cometh unto thee: He is just, and having salvation; lowly, and riding upon an ass, and upon a colt the foal of an ass." Zechariah 9:9

Jesus, Light of the Gentiles..

"And he said, It is a light thing that thou shouldest be my servant to raise up the tribes of Jacob, and to restore the preserved of Israel. I will also give thee for a light to the Gentiles, that thou mayest be my salvation unto the end of the earth. Thus saith the Lord, the Redeemer of Israel, and his Holy One, to him whom man despiseth, to him whom the nation abhorreth, to a servant of rulers, Kings shall see and arise, princes also shall worship, because of the Lord that is faithful, and the Holy One of Israel, and he shall choose thee. Thus saith the Lord, In an acceptable time have I heard thee, and in a day of salvation have I helped thee: and I will preserve thee, and give thee for a covenant of the people, to establish the earth, to cause to inherit the desolate heritages; That thou mayest say to the prisoners, Go forth; to them that are in darkness, Show yourselves. They shall feed in the ways, and their pastures shall be in all high places." Isaiah 49:6-9

Jesus; Light of the World...

"The people walking in darkness have seen a great light; on those living in the land of the shadow of death a light has dawned." Isaiah 9:1

Blind Eyes Shall Be Opened...The Lame Shall Leap...

"See, a King will reign in righteousness and rulers will rule with justice. Each man will be like a shelter from the wind and a refuge from the storm, like streams of water in the desert and the shadow of a great rock in a thirsty land. Then the eyes of those who see will no longer be closed, and the ears of those who hear will listen. The mind of the rash will know and understand, and the stammering tongue will be fluent and clear. No longer will the fool be called noble nor the scoundrel be highly respected." Isaiah 32:1-5

"Say to them that are of a fearful heart, Be strong, fear not: behold, your God will come with vengeance, even God with a recompense; he will come and save you. Then the eyes of the blind shall be opened, and the ears of the deaf shall be unstopped. Then shall the lame man leap as an hart, and the tongue of the dumb sing: for in the wilderness shall waters break out, and streams in the desert. And the parched ground shall become a pool, and the thirsty land springs of water: in the habitation of dragons, where each lay, shall be grass with reeds and rushes. And an highway shall be there, and a way, and it shall be called The way of holiness; the unclean shall not pass over it; but it shall be for those: the wayfaring men, though fools, shall not err therein." Isaiah 35:4-8

Jesus, Man of sorrows...

"Behold, my servant shall deal prudently, he shall be exalted and extolled, and be very high. As many were astonished at thee; his visage was so marred more than any man, and his form more than the sons of men: So shall he sprinkle many nations; the kings shall shut their mouths at him: for that which had not been told them shall they see; and that which they had not heard shall they consider." Isaiah 52:13-15

"Who hath believed our report? and to whom is the arm of the Lord revealed? For he shall grow up before him as a tender plant, and as a root out of a dry ground: he hath no form nor comeliness; and when we shall see him, there is no beauty that we should desire

him. He is despised and rejected of men; a man of sorrows, and acquainted with grief: and we hid as it were our faces from him; he was despised, and we esteemed him not." Isaiah 53:1-3

Jesus, bearing our griefs…

"Surely he hath borne our griefs, and carried our sorrows: yet we did esteem him stricken, smitten of God, and afflicted. But he was wounded for our transgressions, he was bruised for our iniquities: the chastisement of our peace was upon him; and with his stripes we are healed. All we like sheep have gone astray; we have turned every one to his own way; and the Lord hath laid on him the iniquity of us all."
Isaiah 53:4-6

Jesus; crucified for us…

"He was oppressed, and he was afflicted, yet he opened not his mouth: he is brought as a lamb to the slaughter, and as a sheep before her shearers is dumb, so he openeth not his mouth." Isaiah 53:7

"He was taken from prison and from judgment: and who shall declare his generation? for he was cut off out of the land of the living: for the transgression of my people was he stricken. And he made his grave with the wicked, and with the rich in his death; because he had done no violence, neither was any deceit in his mouth.

"Yet it pleased the Lord to bruise him; he hath put him to grief: when thou shalt make his soul an offering for sin, he shall see his seed, he shall prolong his days, and the pleasure of the Lord shall prosper in his hand.

"He shall see of the travail of his soul, and shall be satisfied: by his knowledge shall my righteous servant justify many; for he shall bear their iniquities.

"Therefore will I divide him a portion with the great, and he shall divide the spoil with the strong; because he hath poured out his soul unto death: and he was numbered with the transgressors; and he bare the sin of many, and made intercession for the transgressors."
Isaiah 53:8-12

"For dogs have compassed me: the assembly of the wicked have enclosed me: they pierced my hands and my feet.

I may tell all my bones: they look and stare upon me. They part my garments among them, and cast lots upon my vesture." Psalm 22:16-18

Jesus, risen from the dead…

"Come, and let us return unto the Lord: for he hath torn, and he will heal us; he hath smitten, and he will bind us up. After two days will he revive us: in the third day he will raise us up, and we shall live in his sight. Then shall we know, if we follow on to know the Lord: his going forth is prepared as the morning; and he shall come unto us as the rain, as the latter and former rain unto the earth." Hosea 6:1-3

Pause came when a soft paw gentled Sister's leg, and large, querulous golden eyes gazed up at her.

"Oh Caro! We have let the fire go down, and the room is cold? And you are hungry?"

Time to renew the fire, to stand a wee while in the open doorway, watching the rain slant down in the light, breathing deeply of the cool air, soft on her skin.

To feed the cats and replenish her own body.

Then to sit again by candlelight and firelight.

She fingered a tendril of ivy now, work laid aside, remembering old customs of the "Hanging of the Greens"...

Christmas at Wheatedge

(from "Laicus; or Experiences of a Layman in a Country Parish." By Lyman Abbott)

Is there any reason why Episcopalians, Lutherans and Roman Catholics should have a monopoly of Christmas? Is its glorious old patron Saint partial? Has the Christ-child no gifts for us as well as for other folk? Have the December heavens no brightness-the angel host no song for "blue Presbyterians?"

May we not come to the sacred manger too? Are our Church festivals so many that we need dread to add another? Is our religion so inclined to gayety and money-making that we need curb its joyous tendencies?

The very air of Christmas is marvellous. The heavens are never so blue, the sun never shines with a profuser generosity. The very earth clothes itself in the spotless white of the heavenly robe, as if to prepare for the coming of its Lord.

Alas for him who does not believe in Christmas! May the ghost of Scrooge haunt him into a better mind.

This was what I mentally ejaculated to myself last Saturday afternoon after Mr. Hardcap's protest against our Christmas celebration.

The Sabbath morning previous, Miss Moore came to me mysteriously after church.

"I want to walk home with you, Mr. Laicus," said she.

I have a wife and children, and I felt safe.

"I shall be delighted with the honor," I replied.

But Miss Moore's honors are never empty ones. I knew that she wanted something; I wondered what. I had not long to wonder; for we had not crossed the road before she opened the subject.

"We are going to trim the Church for Christmas," said she, "and we want you to superintend getting the evergreens."

"What?" said I, aghast.

Confidentially, please not mention it, I have been in the habit for a good many years of taking my wife and my prayer-book to the Episcopal Church on Christmas-day. Dickens converted me to its observance ten years or more ago. But none are so sound as those who are tinged with heresy. And am I not a "blue Presbyterian?" It would not do to lend my countenance too readily to indecorous invasions of the sanctuary with festivals borrowed from the Roman Catholics.

Besides, what would the elders say? I asked Miss Moore as much.

"Deacon Goodsole will lend us his pung," was the reply.

"And the trustees?" said I.

But Miss Moore never leaves a point unguarded.

"Young Wheaton is home from school," said she, "and he will go with you to the woods. He will call to-morrow, right after breakfast."

For a difficult piece of generalship give me a woman. Not fitted for politics! Why, they are born to it. Here was Miss Moore bent on trimming the church. And lawyer Laicus was to go in Deacon Goodsole's sleigh with the son of the President of the Board of Trustees to get the "trimmings." He who dares to complain after that enlists two dignitaries and one very respectable layman against him at the outset.

"Very well," said I, "I will go."

"Go!" said Miss Moore, "of course you'll go. Nobody doubted that. But I want to tell you where to go and what to get."

The next morning I was just finishing my second cup of coffee when I heard the jingle of bells, and, looking up, saw Jim Wheaton and the Deacon's sleek horse at my door. So, bidding Harry, who was to go too, "be quick," an exhortation that needed no repeating, we were very soon in the pung, armed I with a hatchet, Harry with a pruning knife.

That ride was one to be remembered. The air was crisp and clear. Just snow enough had fallen in the night to cover every black and noisome thing, as though all nature's sins were washed away by her Sabbath repentance, and she had commenced her life afresh.

There was luxury in every inhalation of the pure air.

The horse, more impatient than we, could scarcely wait for leave to go, and needed no word thereafter to quicken his flying feet. Down the hill, with merry ringing bells, ever and anon showered with flying snow from the horse's hoof; through the village street with a nod of recognition to Deacon Goodsole, who stood at his door to wave us a cheery recognition; round the corner with a whirl that threatens to deposit us in the soft snow and leave the horse with an empty sleigh; across the bridge, which spans the creek; up, with unabated speed, the little hill on the other side;

across the railroad track, with real commiseration for the travelers who are trotting up and down the platform waiting for the train, and must exchange the joyous freedom of this day for the treadmill of the city, this air for that smoke and gas, this clean pure mantle of snow for that fresh accumulation of sooty sloshy filth; pass the school-house, where the gathering scholars stand, snowballs in hand, to see us run merrily by, one urchin, more mischievous than the rest, sending a ball whizzing after us; up, up, up the mountain road, for half a mile, past farm-houses whose curling smoke tell of great blazing fires within; past ricks of hay all robed in white, and one ghost of a last summer's scare-crow watching still, though the corn is long since in-gathered and the crows have long since flown to warmer climes;

turning off, at last, from the highway into Squire Wheaton's wood road, where, since the last fall of snow, nothing has been before us, save a solitary rabbit whose track our dog Jip follows excitedly, till he is quite out of sight or even call.

Here we are at last. And here the evergeens are about us in a profusion which would make the eyes water of my honest friend the Dutch grocer who supplied me with my family trees so many years in New York. Our smoking nag is over his impatience now, and, being well blanketed, understands what is wanted of him quite as well as if he were tied, and stands as still as if he were Squire Slowgoes' fat and lazy "family horse." With pants tied snugly over our topboots to keep out the intruding snow, we plunge into the woods.

The ringing blows of our hatchets on the cedar-trees bring down a mimic shower on our heads and backs. Young Wheaton understands his business, and shows me how the fairest evergreens are hid beneath the snow, and what rare forms of crystalline beauty conceal themselves altogether beneath this white counterpane. So, sometimes cutting from above and sometimes grubbing from below, we work an hour or more, till our pung is filled to its brim. Long before we have finished Jip has returned from his useless search, and the neighing horse indicates his impatience to be off again.

When we got back to the Church we found it warm with a blazing fire in the great stove, and bright with a bevy of laughing girls, who emptied our sleigh of its contents almost before we were aware what had happened, and were impatiently demanding more. Miss Moore had proposed just to trim the pulpit-oh! but she is a shrewd manager-and we had brought evergreens enough to make two or three. But the plans had grown faster by far than we could work. One young lady had remarked how beautiful the chandelier would look with an evergreen wreath; a second had pointed out that there ought to be large festoons draping the windows; a third, the soprano, had declared that the choir had as good a right to trimming as the pulpit; a fourth, a graduate of Mount Holyoke, had proposed some mottoes, and had agreed to cut the letters, and Mr. Leacock, the store keeper, had been foraged on for pasteboard, and an extemporized table contrived on which to cut and trim them.

So off we were driven again, with barely time to thaw out our half-frozen toes; and, in short, my half morning's job lengthened out to a long day's hard but joyous work, before the pile of evergreens in the hall was large enough to supply the energies of the Christmas workers.

Of course, we must trim the Sunday school-room as well as the Church, for the children must have their Christmas; and trimmed it was, so luxuriantly that it seemed as though the woods had laid siege to and taken possession of the sanctuary, and that nature was preparing to join on this glad day her voice with that of man in singing praise to Him who brings life to a winter-wrapped earth, and whose fittest symbol, therefore, is the tree whose greenness not even the frosts of the coldest winter have power to diminish.

Of course Christmas itself passed without recognition. I went, as is my wont, with my wife and my prayer-book, to the Episcopal Church.

Our Christmas waited till Sunday. A glorious day it was. The sun never shone more brightly. The crisp keenness was gone from the air. The balmy breath of spring was in it. The Church never was so full before and never has been since. The story of its decorations had been spread far and wide, and all Wheathedge flocked to see what the Presbyterians would make of Christmas. The pulpit, the walls, the gallery, the chandelier were festooned with wreaths of living green.

A cross-O tempora! O mores!-of cedar and immortelles, stood on the communion table. Over the pulpit were those sublime words of the sublimest of all books, "He shall save His people from their sins."

Opposite it, emblazoned on the gallery, was heaven and earth's fitting response to this sublime revelation,

"Glory be to God on high."

Miss Moore was better than her word. She managed both choir and minister. Both were in the spirit of the occasion. The parson never preached a better sermon than his Christmas meditation. The choir never sung a more joyous song of praise than their Christmas anthem. And before the influence of that morning's service I think the last objection to observing Christmas faded out.

For there had been some objections. I heard of two.

One came from Mr. Wheaton. Monday afternoon, going by the Church, he saw the door open, went in, found it full of busy workers; ceiling, aisles, pulpit, and gallery, strewed with evergreens, and the clatter of merry voices keeping pace with the busy fingers. It was his first intimation of what was going on.

"Heyday!" said he. "What is all this? Who authorized it, I should like to know?"

The chatter of merry voices ceased. The young ladies were in awe. Miss Moore was not there to answer for them. No one dared act as spokesman. Young Jim Wheaton was on a step-ladder rather dangerously resting on the backs of two pews. He was tacking the letter G to the gallery. He noticed the silence and discerned the cause.

"Father," said he, "I wish you would hold this ladder for me a minute. It is rather ticklish."

"Ah, Jim, is that you?" said the old man. Pride in Jim is the father's weak point. The ladder was held. Then his advice was asked about the placing of the mottoes; and it was given, and that was the last of Mr. Wheaton's objection.

The other objection came from Mr. Hardcap, the carpenter. I met him at the door of the church Saturday afternoon, just as the last rubbish had been swept out and we were closing the door.

"Looks beautiful, doesn't it Mr. Hardcap?" said I.

"They'd better have spent their time on their knees than with these fixins," growled Mr. Hardcap; "'twould ha' done the Church more good, a deal sight."

"Did you spend your time on your knees?" I could not refrain from asking.

But Mr. Hardcap did not answer.

Sister smiled at the bright warmth the words created.

At the unbending of the hardest heart.

When the Light shines with joy and brightness.

Catching fire in every heart.

Early darkness, after a clear, calm day.

Sister had walked long on the pale golden shore, watching the seals, singing carols to them in the bright sun.

Gathering driftwood that would flame blue with the salt in it.

And now, her hands were restless, seeking some new occupation.

Before the order of knitting she was expecting arrived.

"Oh, I know! It is so long since I did any embroidery."

There were just a very, very few she needed to send cards to, so this year she would embroider them.

So she fetched the old work basket where oddments of material and threads lay.

Her hands instinctively sought white linen, and red and green thread, and she remembered something she had written years before as she threaded a needle.

The Colours of Christmas

Red, green, white... The colours of Christmas!

Poinsettias, scarlet against green... Christmas trees, evergreen...holly, dark, glossy green with bright red berries...fireglow...mistletoe, white berries, whitest snow...

These are the colours of Christmas, traditional, inbuilt...

One of the oldest carols; "The holly bears a berry, as red as any blood"...

And the old carols, singing evocatively of apple trees, of cherries…of snow...

The colours of Christmas, red, green, white... Green; growing, springing... renewing…changing…

Red...life-birthing, life-ending.

Green wood, chiseled and sawn into a manger ...and a cross...

But no! You cry?

This is a family time?

A warm and glowing time? For peace and comfort, feasting,
love; all things pretty?

Not for death!

And, yes, it is that, all of that - but so much more than that.

Comfort that is real and lasting, rather than illusory and cloying, needs must be founded on and grounded in truth and that fullness of reality that is truth.

For if we accept the gold, but not the myrrh, see the pretty baby, but not the pains of that bitter birth, surrounded with rejection and social stigma?

See the Baby-Who-is-God, but not the Man -Who -Dies-as God?

We then deny the huge gift given, weaken the grace...trivialise and tame that breathing Spirit, limit and deny God...

Babies; so utterly vulnerable and needy. So defenceless, and defended.

God, in that wooden manger, eliciting and evoking the deepest instincts in us. And that birth but a beginning, but one stage, begun in the dark warmth of Mary's womb, of a life made to be given fully, in living, but above all in dying.

If it were not for the dying, there would be no rejoicing or thanksgiving in the birthing.

Are we content to accept Him as that baby, accept Him as a vulnerable youngling?

But not as the One-Who-Died our human death, rejected and scorned?

Whose coming in our flesh saved us from all the ills and wrongs done by that flesh?

For every birth is a death too; for death is an integral part of human life - the life that God sanctified by entering into its joys and its pains, all of them from conception to death.

We change; we grow. Baby into child into man... tree into green leaf, then into red berry, and into manger and cross.

Tiny stitches, criss-crossing white fabric with scarlet and green.

The colours of Christmas. The green of promise; the crimson of fulfilment.

In the old carols, the red of cherries and of apples...the green of tree and holly.

Maybe simply we have lost touch so much with these realities, this rich mingling of life with death, that these things shock and disturb us?

In times past, masters who painted the Nativity invariably put a crucifix into the scene.

The baby defeats death; thus the deep joy... God does not deny death; He conquers it. The cost is blood, His blood.

So; we rejoice, and are at peace.

We revel in the baby born; knowing that He will die as we die - but not the death that was before He came.

The colours of Christmas… Green growing, red blossoming and fruiting. The pure, white light of the truth and love of God shining out through that baby, through that star.

And shining out to others through each one of us who accepts and embraces Jesus, baby, man, Saviour, Spouse.

Shining clear and strong out into a dark world, spilling light as He spilled His blood.

Candles that are consumed as they shine out for others.

That gift is a challenge. Accepting it will change your life, take you down paths you had not thought to take...

Through the green leafy glades to the scarlet blossoms... Through life - and through death.

And whatever we give in response to that love, in time, in energy, in skills, in money, is so little against what we are given.

We give not out of obligation or obedience, not constrained or forced, but in sheer exuberant joy and freedom!

That freedom that He gives us in His giving of His life in love for us. So we give our lives as He gave His, and the love spreads outwards, light radiating into darkness.

Even as the candles burn away they glow warmth and light.

The colours of Christmas… patterned green and red stitches on pure white; tiny crosses, tiny hopes, tiny shoots and fruits.

The fire burned low now, and the candle too...

And in the next days, peace settled on the small old cottage...

Advent ripened and grew... and time for thinking ahead to some of the traditional foods.

Stir up Sunday!!

And memories of spices and dried fruits.

Essence of Christmas!

Rich aromas rising from Sister's kitchen as she mixed mincemeat to mature gently.

And all the old customs running through her mind... Of how mince pies use to be oval, to represent the Crib… Until the Puritans shook their fists in horror and banned this…terrible custom!

Sister had found oval moulds of course.

So she would shape the small delicacies, full of such riches…

And cut tiny pastry stars to go atop them.

Remembering days on the island, when she had made an apple pie for the postman, each Christmas, decorating it with pastry stars and doves. For he was a man on his own.

But that was for the future... For now, enough to mix and spice, with Caro, whose tastes in food were eccentric and eclectic, sitting at her feet watching her every move.

Thoughtfully mouthing a sultana she "accidentally" dropped by his feet.

And she read of other festive specialities also.

Of the huge puddings made in the workhouses, enough for 300 people.

She had visited a ruined workhouse and seen the huge hearth with the great cauldron set on stones above the fire.

Crude but effective.

And it had rejoiced her heart to read of the preparations and celebrations arranged for the inmates.

Of the feast of roast beef, plum pudding and good beer or porter. Of tobacco and snuff, of fruit and biscuits and sweets for the children. Respite from the usual meagre diet.

And she remembered the "clootie dumplings" of island days, a rich concoction slightly less rich than traditional Christmas puddings, for it had been made not for the latterly-come season, but for Hogmanay.

And the first time she had made one, and forgotten to leave room for the chemical reaction that made the cloth-wrapped pudding rise and swell... Her hens had enjoyed the resulting fruity soup, and she had remained thankful that the lid had been firmly on the pan.

So many seemingly small and ordinary items drawn into the symbolism.

So an orange became the foundation for the Christingle.

A wry smile as she remembered, long ago now, a dear old lady who had been a girl in the last War, when oranges were never seen. And when frugality was a part of life perforce.

When they had had a Christingle service at her Church, she had lamented loudly at the waste of a good orange, as it was made unfit to eat.

Sister had had a hard time assuring her that the custom had begin with an orange that was overripe…

But it was a pretty idea.

And one that the smallest child could make.

A red ribbon, for the Blood of Jesus, around the round world of the orange.

That also showed the fruitfulness of the world.

Four small sticks, for the four seasons, with dried fruit or small sweets threaded on, for the fruitfulness of the world.

And atop, firmly rooted, a candle for the Light of Christ.

A section pared off the bottom of the orange made a stand.

And with that sweet thought, Sister wended her way to bed.

The Third Verse...

What can I give Him, poor as I am?
If I were a shepherd,
I would bring a lamb.

If I were a Wise Man,
I would play my part.

Yet what I can I give him,
Give my heart.

Living the Light...

Ah the stories!

Sister built the fire high now, settling in for the evening before Christmas Eve, to read, and enjoy the quiet hours.

All four candles burned strong and true... and tomorrow night the pure white Light would shine.

The wee cottage shone and sparkled. All was ready.

Fulfilment in the giving, in the Gift.

And ah! All the stories.

Inspired and inspiring.

Old favourites re-read, and many pondered differently on.

Not great, rich displays. No fireworks or fanfares.

Simply people, living their love in their often slender means. Within what they had and were.

And here they were, the ones that spoke to the mind and soul most…

The Gift of the Magi,
by O'Henry.

One dollar and eighty-seven cents. That was all. And sixty cents of it was in pennies. Pennies saved one and two at a time by bulldozing the grocer and the vegetable man and the butcher until one's cheeks burned with the silent imputation of parsimony that such close dealing implied. Three times Della counted it. One dollar and eighty-seven cents. And the next day would be Christmas.

There was clearly nothing to do but flop down on the shabby little couch and howl. So Della did it. Which instigates the moral reflection that life is made up of sobs, sniffles, and smiles, with sniffles predominating.

While the mistress of the home is gradually subsiding from the first stage to the second, take a look at the home. A furnished flat at $8 per week. It did not exactly beggar description, but it certainly had that word on the lookout for the mendicancy squad.

In the vestibule below was a letter-box into which no letter would go, and an electric button from which no mortal finger could coax a ring. Also appertaining thereunto was a card bearing the name "Mr. James Dillingham Young." The "Dillingham" had been flung to the breeze during a former period of prosperity when its possessor was being paid $30 per week. Now, when the income was shrunk to $20, though, they were thinking seriously of contracting to a modest and unassuming D. But whenever Mr. James Dillingham Young came home and reached his flat above he was called "Jim" and greatly hugged by Mrs. James Dillingham Young, already introduced to you as Della. Which is all very good.

Della finished her cry and attended to her cheeks with the powder rag. She stood by the window and looked out dully at a gray cat walking a gray fence in a gray backyard.

Tomorrow would be Christmas Day, and she had only $1.87 with which to buy Jim a present. She had been saving every penny she could for months, with this result. Twenty dollars a week doesn't go far. Expenses had been greater than she had calculated. They always are. Only $1.87 to buy a present for Jim. Her Jim. Many a happy hour she had spent planning for something nice for him. Something fine and rare and sterling--something just a little bit near to being worthy of the honor of being owned by Jim.

There was a pier-glass between the windows of the room. Perhaps you have seen a pierglass in an $8 flat. A very thin and very agile person may, by observing his reflection in a rapid sequence of longitudinal strips, obtain a fairly accurate conception of his looks. Della, being slender, had mastered the art.

Suddenly she whirled from the window and stood before the glass. Her eyes were shining brilliantly, but her face had lost its color within twenty seconds. Rapidly she pulled down her hair and let it fall to its full length.

Now, there were two possessions of the James Dillingham Youngs in which they both took a mighty pride. One was Jim's gold watch that had been his father's and his grandfather's. The other was Della's hair. Had the queen of Sheba lived in the flat across the airshaft, Della would have let her hair hang out the window some day to dry just to depreciate Her Majesty's jewels and gifts. Had King Solomon been the janitor, with all his treasures piled up in the basement, Jim would have pulled out his watch every time he passed, just to see him pluck at his beard from envy.

So now Della's beautiful hair fell about her rippling and shining like a cascade of brown waters. It reached below her knee and made itself almost a garment for her. And then she did it up again nervously and quickly. Once she faltered for a minute and stood still while a tear or two splashed on the worn red carpet.

On went her old brown jacket; on went her old brown hat. With a whirl of skirts and with the brilliant sparkle still in her eyes, she fluttered out the door and down the stairs to the street.

Where she stopped the sign read: "Mne. Sofronie. Hair Goods of All Kinds."

One flight up Della ran, and collected herself, panting. Madame, large, too white, chilly, hardly looked the "Sofronie."

"Will you buy my hair?" asked Della.

"I buy hair," said Madame. "Take yer hat off and let's have a sight at the looks of it."

Down rippled the brown cascade.

"Twenty dollars," said Madame, lifting the mass with a practised hand.

"Give it to me quick," said Della.

Oh, and the next two hours tripped by on rosy wings. Forget the hashed metaphor. She was ransacking the stores for Jim's present.

She found it at last. It surely had been made for Jim and no one else. There was no other like it in any of the stores, and she had turned all of them inside out. It was a platinum fob chain simple and chaste in design, properly proclaiming its value by substance alone and not by meretricious ornamentation—as all good things should do. It was even worthy of The Watch. As soon as she saw it she knew that it must be Jim's. It was like him. Quietness and value—the description applied to both. Twenty-one dollars they took from her for it, and she hurried home with the 87 cents. With that chain on his watch Jim might be properly anxious about the time in any company. Grand as the watch was, he sometimes looked at it on the sly on account of the old leather strap that he used in place of a chain.

When Della reached home her intoxication gave way a little to prudence and reason. She got out her curling irons and lighted the gas and went to work repairing the ravages made by generosity added to love. Which is always a tremendous task, dear friends—a mammoth task.

Within forty minutes her head was covered with tiny, close-lying curls that made her look wonderfully like a truant schoolboy. She looked at her reflection in the mirror long, carefully, and critically.

"If Jim doesn't kill me," she said to herself, "before he takes a second look at me, he'll say I look like a Coney Island chorus girl. But what could I do—oh! what could I do with a dollar and eighty-seven cents?"

At 7 o'clock the coffee was made and the frying-pan was on the back of the stove hot and ready to cook the chops.

Jim was never late. Della doubled the fob chain in her hand and sat on the corner of the table near the door that he always entered. Then she heard his step on the stair away down on the first flight, and she turned white for just a moment. She had a habit of saying a little silent prayer about the simplest everyday things, and now she whispered: "Please God, make him think I am still pretty."

The door opened and Jim stepped in and closed it. He looked thin and very serious. Poor fellow, he was only twenty-two—and to be burdened with a family! He needed a new overcoat and he was without gloves.

Jim stopped inside the door, as immovable as a setter at the scent of quail. His eyes were fixed upon Della, and there was an expression in them that she could not read, and it terrified her. It was not anger, nor surprise, nor disapproval, nor horror, nor any of the sentiments that she had been prepared for. He simply stared at her fixedly with that peculiar expression on his face.

Della wriggled off the table and went for him.

"Jim, darling," she cried, "don't look at me that way. "I had my hair cut off and sold because I couldn't have lived through Christmas without giving you a present. It'll grow out again—you won't mind, will you? I just had to do it. My hair grows awfully fast. Say

'Merry Christmas!' Jim, and let's be happy. You don't know what a nice—what a beautiful, nice gift I've got for you."

"You've cut off your hair?" asked Jim, laboriously, as if he had not arrived at that patent fact yet even after the hardest mental labor.

"Cut it off and sold it," said Della. "Don't you like me just as well, anyhow? I'm me without my hair, ain't I?"

Jim looked about the room curiously.

"You say your hair is gone?" he said, with an air almost of idiocy.

"You needn't look for it," said Della. "It's sold, I tell you—sold and gone, too. It's Christmas Eve, boy. Be good to me, for it went for you. Maybe the hairs of my head were numbered," she went on with sudden serious sweetness, "but nobody could ever count my love for you. Shall I put the chops on, Jim?"

Out of his trance Jim seemed quickly to wake. He enfolded his Della. For ten seconds let us regard with discreet scrutiny some inconsequential object in the other direction. Eight dollars a week or a million a year—what is the difference? A mathematician or a wit would give you the wrong answer. The magi brought valuable gifts, but that was not among them. This dark assertion will be illuminated later on.

Jim drew a package from his overcoat pocket and threw it upon the table.

"Don't make any mistake, Dell," he said, "about me. I don't think there's anything in the way of a haircut or a shave or a shampoo that could make me like my girl any less. But if you'll unwrap that package you may see why you had me going a while at first."

White fingers and nimble tore at the string and paper. And then an ecstatic scream of joy; and then, alas! a quick feminine change to hysterical tears and wails, necessitating the immediate employment of all the comforting powers of the lord of the flat.

For there lay The Combs—the set of combs, side and back, that Della had worshipped long in a Broadway window. Beautiful combs, pure tortoise shell, with jeweled rims—just the shade to wear in the beautiful vanished hair. They were expensive combs, she knew, and her heart had simply craved and yearned over them without the least hope of possession. And now, they were hers, but the tresses that should have adorned the coveted adornments were gone.

But she hugged them to her bosom, and at length she was able to look up with dim eyes and a smile and say: "My hair grows so fast, Jim!"

And then Della leaped up like a little singed cat and cried, "Oh, oh!"

Jim had not yet seen his beautiful present. She held it out to him eagerly upon her open palm. The dull precious metal seemed to flash with a reflection of her bright and ardent spirit.

"Isn't it a dandy, Jim? I hunted all over town to find it. You'll have to look at the time a hundred times a day now. Give me your watch. I want to see how it looks on it."

Instead of obeying, Jim tumbled down on the couch and put his hands under the back of his head and smiled.

"Dell," said he, "let's put our Christmas presents away and keep 'em a while. They're too nice to use just at present. I sold the watch to get the money to buy your combs. And now suppose you put the chops on."

The magi, as you know, were wise men—wonderfully wise men—who brought gifts to the Babe in the manger. They invented the art of giving Christmas presents. Being wise, their gifts were no doubt wise ones, possibly bearing the privilege of exchange in case of duplication. And here I have lamely related to you the uneventful chronicle of two foolish children in a flat who most unwisely sacrificed for each other the greatest treasures of their house. But in a last word to the wise of these days let it be said that of all who give gifts these two were the wisest. Of all who give and receive gifts, such as they are wisest. Everywhere they are wisest. They are the magi.

From "A Christmas Carol" by Charles Dickens.

Scrooge is taken in hand by the Spirit of Christmas Present...

They stood in the city streets on Christmas morning, where (for the weather was severe) the people made a rough, but brisk and not unpleasant kind of music, in scraping the snow from the pavement in front of their dwellings, and from the tops of their houses, whence it was mad delight to the boys to see it come plumping down into the road below, and splitting into artificial little snow-storms.

The house fronts looked black enough, and the windows blacker, contrasting with the smooth white sheet of snow upon the roofs, and with the dirtier snow upon the ground; which last deposit had been ploughed up in deep furrows by the heavy wheels of carts and wagons; furrows that crossed and recrossed each other hundreds of times where the great streets branched off, and made intricate channels, hard to trace in the thick yellow mud and icy water. The sky was gloomy, and the shortest streets were choked up with a dingy mist, half thawed, half frozen, whose heavier particles descended in shower of sooty atoms, as if all the chimneys in Great Britain had, by one consent, caught fire, and were blazing away to their dear hearts' content. There was nothing very cheerful in the climate or the town, and yet was there an air of cheerfulness abroad that the clearest summer air and brightest summer sun might have endeavoured to diffuse in vain.

For, the people who were shovelling away on the housetops were jovial and full of glee; calling out to one another from the parapets, and now and then exchanging a facetious snowball -- better-natured missile far than many a wordy jest -- laughing heartily if it went right and not less heartily if it went wrong. The poulterers' shops were still half open, and the fruiterers' were radiant in their glory. There were great, round, pot-bellied baskets of chestnuts, shaped like the waistcoats of jolly old gentlemen, lolling at the doors, and tumbling out into the street in their apoplectic opulence. There were ruddy, brown-faced, broad-girthed Spanish Friars, and winking from their shelves in wanton slyness at the girls as they went by, and glanced demurely at the hung-up mistletoe. There were pears and apples, clustered high in blooming pyramids; there were bunches of grapes, made, in the shopkeepers' benevolence to dangle from conspicuous hooks, that people's mouths might water gratis as they passed; there were piles of filberts, mossy and brown, recalling, in their fragrance, ancient walks among the woods, and pleasant shufflings ankle deep through withered leaves; there were Norfolk Biffins, squab and swarthy, setting off the yellow of the oranges and lemons, and, in the great compactness of their juicy persons, urgently entreating and beseeching to be carried home in paper bags and eaten after dinner. The very gold and silver fish, set forth among these choice fruits in a bowl, though members of a dull and stagnant-blooded race, appeared to know that there was something going on; and, to a fish, went gasping round and round their little world in slow and passionless excitement.

The Grocers'! oh the Grocers'! Nearly closed, with perhaps two shutters down, or one; but through those gaps such glimpses. It was not alone that the scales descending on the counter made a merry sound, or that the twine and roller parted company so briskly, or that the canisters were rattled up and down like juggling tricks, or even that the blended scents of tea and coffee were so grateful to the nose, or even that the raisins were so plentiful and rare, the almonds so extremely white, the sticks of cinnamon so long and straight, the other spices so delicious, the candied fruits so caked and spotted with molten sugar as to make the coldest lookers-on feel faint and subsequently bilious. Nor was it that the figs were moist and pulpy, or that the French plums blushed in modest tartness from their highly-decorated boxes, or that everything was good to eat and in its Christmas dress; but the customers were all so hurried and so eager in the hopeful promise of the day, that they tumbled up against each other at the door, clashing their wicker baskets wildly, and left their purchases upon the counter, and came running back to fetch them, and committed hundreds of the like mistakes, in the best humour possible; while the Grocer and his people were so frank and fresh that the polished hearts with which they fastened their aprons behind might have been their own, worn outside for general inspection, and for Christmas daws to peck at if they chose.

But soon the steeples called good people all, to church and chapel, and away they came, flocking through the streets in their best clothes, and with their gayest faces. And at the same time there emerged from scores of bye-streets, lanes, and nameless turnings, innumerable people, carrying their dinners to the bakers' shops. The sight of these poor revellers appeared to interest the Spirit very much, for he stood with Scrooge beside him in a baker's doorway, and taking off the covers as their bearers passed, sprinkled incense on their dinners from his torch. And it was a very uncommon kind of torch, for once or twice when there were angry words between some dinner-carriers who had jostled each other, he shed a few drops of water on them from it, and their good humour was restored directly. For they said, it was a shame to quarrel upon Christmas Day. And so it was. God love it, so it was.

In time the bells ceased, and the bakers were shut up; and yet there was a genial shadowing forth of all these dinners and the progress of their cooking, in the thawed blotch of wet above each baker's oven; where the pavement smoked as if its stones were cooking too.

"Is there a peculiar flavour in what you sprinkle from your torch?" asked Scrooge.

"There is. My own."

"Would it apply to any kind of dinner on this day?" asked Scrooge.

"To any kindly given. To a poor one most."

"Why to a poor one most?" asked Scrooge.

"Because it needs it most."

They went on, invisible, as they had been before, into the suburbs of the town. It was a remarkable quality of the Ghost (which Scrooge had observed at the baker's), that notwithstanding his gigantic size, he could accommodate himself to any place with ease; and that he stood beneath a low roof quite as gracefully and like a supernatural creature, as it was possible he could have done in any lofty hall.

And perhaps it was the pleasure the good Spirit had in showing off this power of his, or else it was his own kind, generous, hearty nature, and his sympathy with all poor men, that led him straight to Scrooge's clerk's; for there he went, and took Scrooge with him, holding to his robe; and on the threshold of the door the Spirit smiled, and stopped to bless Bob Cratchit's dwelling with the sprinkling of his torch. Think of that. Bob had but fifteen bob a-week himself; he pocketed on Saturdays but fifteen copies of his Christian name; and yet the Ghost of Christmas Present blessed his four-roomed house.

Then up rose Mrs. Cratchit, Cratchit's wife, dressed out but poorly in a twice-turned gown, but brave in ribbons, which are cheap and make a goodly show for sixpence; and she laid the cloth, assisted by Belinda Cratchit, second of her daughters, also brave in ribbons; while Master Peter Cratchit plunged a fork into the saucepan of potatoes, and getting the corners of his monstrous shirt collar (Bob's private property, conferred upon his son and heir in honour of the day) into his mouth, rejoiced to find himself so gallantly attired, and yearned to show his linen in the fashionable Parks. And now two smaller Cratchits, boy and girl, came tearing in, screaming that outside the baker's they had smelt the goose, and known it for their own; and basking in luxurious thoughts of sage and onion, these young Cratchits danced about the table, and exalted Master Peter Cratchit to the skies, while he (not proud, although his collars nearly choked him) blew the fire, until the slow potatoes bubbling up, knocked loudly at the saucepan-lid to be let out and peeled.

"What has ever got your precious father then?" said Mrs. Cratchit. "And your brother, Tiny Tim; And Martha warn't as late last Christmas Day by half-an-hour."

"Here's Martha, mother," said a girl, appearing as she spoke.

"Here's Martha, mother!" cried the two young Cratchits. "Hurrah! There's such a goose, Martha!"

"Why, bless your heart alive, my dear, how late you are!" said Mrs. Cratchit, kissing her a dozen times, and taking off her shawl and bonnet for her with officious zeal.

"We'd a deal of work to finish up last night," replied the girl, "and had to clear away this morning, mother."

"Well. Never mind so long as you are come," said Mrs. Cratchit. "Sit ye down before the fire, my dear, and have a warm, Lord bless ye."

"No, no. There's father coming," cried the two young Cratchits, who were everywhere at once. "Hide, Martha, hide!"

So Martha hid herself, and in came little Bob, the father, with at least three feet of comforter exclusive of the fringe, hanging down before him; and his threadbare clothes darned up and brushed, to look seasonable; and Tiny Tim upon his shoulder. Alas for Tiny Tim, he bore a little crutch, and had his limbs supported by an iron frame.

"Why, where's our Martha?" cried Bob Cratchit, looking round.

"Not coming," said Mrs. Cratchit.

"Not coming!" said Bob, with a sudden declension in his high spirits; for he had been Tim's blood horse all the way from church, and had come home rampant. "Not coming upon Christmas Day?"

Martha didn't like to see him disappointed, if it were only in joke; so she came out prematurely from behind the closet door, and ran into his arms, while the two young Cratchits hustled Tiny Tim, and bore him off into the wash-house, that he might hear the pudding singing in the copper.

"And how did little Tim behave?" asked Mrs. Cratchit, when she had rallied

Bob on his credulity, and Bob had hugged his daughter to his heart's content.

"As good as gold," said Bob, "and better. Somehow he gets thoughtful sitting by himself so much, and thinks the strangest things you ever heard. He told me, coming home, that he hoped the people saw him in the church, because he was a cripple, and it might be pleasant to them to remember upon Christmas Day, who made lame beggars walk, and blind men see."

Bob's voice was tremulous when he told them this, and trembled more when he said that Tiny Tim was growing strong and hearty.

His active little crutch was heard upon the floor, and back came Tiny Tim before another word was spoken, escorted by his brother and sister to his stool before the fire; and while Bob, turning up his cuffs -- as if, poor fellow, they were capable of being made more shabby -- compounded some hot mixture in a jug with gin and lemons, and stirred it round and round and put it on the hob to simmer; Master Peter, and the two ubiquitous young Cratchits went to fetch the goose, with which they soon returned in high procession.

Such a bustle ensued that you might have thought a goose the rarest of all birds; a feathered phenomenon, to which a black swan was a matter of course -- and in truth it was something very like it in that house. Mrs. Cratchit made the gravy (ready beforehand in a little saucepan) hissing hot; Master Peter mashed the potatoes with incredible vigour; Miss Belinda sweetened up the apple-sauce; Martha dusted the hot plates; Bob took Tiny Tim beside him in a tiny corner at the table; the two young Cratchits set chairs for everybody, not forgetting themselves, and mounting guard upon their posts, crammed spoons into their mouths, lest they should shriek for goose before their turn came to be helped. At last the dishes were set on, and grace was said. It was succeeded by a breathless pause, as Mrs. Cratchit, looking slowly all along the carving-knife, prepared to plunge it in the breast; but when she did, and when the long expected gush of stuffing issued forth, one murmur of delight arose all round the board, and even Tiny Tim, excited by the two young Cratchits, beat on the table with the handle of his knife, and feebly cried Hurrah!

There never was such a goose. Bob said he didn't believe there ever was such a goose cooked. Its tenderness and flavour, size and cheapness, were the themes of universal admiration. Eked out by apple-sauce and mashed potatoes, it was a sufficient dinner for the whole family; indeed, as Mrs. Cratchit said with great delight (surveying one small atom of a bone upon the dish), they hadn't ate it all at last. Yet every one had had enough, and the youngest Cratchits in particular, were steeped in sage and onion to the eyebrows. But now, the plates being changed by Miss Belinda, Mrs. Cratchit left the room alone -- too nervous to bear witnesses -- to take the pudding up and bring it in.

Suppose it should not be done enough? Suppose it should break in turning out? Suppose somebody should have got over the wall of the back-yard, and stolen it, while they were merry with the goose -- a supposition at which the two young Cratchits became livid? All sorts of horrors were supposed.

Hallo! A great deal of steam! The pudding was out of the copper. A smell like a washing-day. That was the cloth. A smell like an eating-house and a pastrycook's next door to each other, with a laundress's next door to that. That was the pudding. In half a minute Mrs. Cratchit entered -- flushed, but smiling proudly -- with the pudding, like a speckled cannon-ball, so hard and firm, blazing in half of half-a-quartern of ignited brandy, and bedight with Christmas holly stuck into the top.

Oh, a wonderful pudding! Bob Cratchit said, and calmly too, that he regarded it as the greatest success achieved by Mrs. Cratchit since their marriage. Mrs. Cratchit said that now the weight was off her mind, she would confess she had had her doubts about the quantity of flour. Everybody had something to say about it, but nobody said or thought it was at all a small pudding for a large family. It would have been flat heresy to do so. Any Cratchit would have blushed to hint at such a thing.

At last the dinner was all done, the cloth was cleared, the hearth swept, and the fire made up. The compound in the jug being tasted, and considered perfect, apples and oranges were put upon the table, and a shovel-full of chestnuts on the fire. Then all the Cratchit family drew round the hearth, in what Bob Cratchit called a circle, meaning half a one; and at Bob Cratchit's elbow stood the family display of glass. Two tumblers, and a custard-cup without a handle.

These held the hot stuff from the jug, however, as well as golden goblets would have done; and Bob served it out with beaming looks, while the chestnuts on the fire sputtered and cracked noisily. Then Bob proposed: "A Merry Christmas to us all, my dears. God bless us."

Which all the family re-echoed.

"God bless us every one!" said Tiny Tim, the last of all.

"God Bless Us, Every One!"

From "Little Women" by Louisa M. Alcott

"Christmas won't be Christmas without any presents," grumbled Jo, lying on the rug.

"It's so dreadful to be poor!" sighed Meg, looking down at her old dress.

"I don't think it's fair for some girls to have plenty of pretty things, and other girls nothing at all," added little Amy, with an injured sniff.

"We've got Father and Mother, and each other," said Beth contentedly from her corner.

The four young faces on which the firelight shone brightened at the cheerful words, but darkened again as Jo said sadly, "We haven't got Father, and shall not have him for a long time."

She didn't say, "Perhaps never," but each silently added it, thinking of Father far away, where the fighting was.

Nobody spoke for a minute; then Meg said in an altered tone, "You know the reason Mother proposed not having any presents this Christmas was because it is going to be a hard winter for everyone; and she thinks we ought not to spend money for pleasure, when our men are suffering so in the army. We can't do much, but we can make our little sacrifices, and ought to do it gladly. But I am afraid I don't," and Meg shook her head, as she thought regretfully of all the pretty things she wanted.

"But I don't think the little we should spend would do any good. We've each got a dollar, and the army wouldn't be much helped by our giving that. I agree not to expect anything from Mother or you, but I do want to buy 'Undine and Sintran' for myself. I've wanted it so long," said Jo, who was a bookworm.

"I planned to spend mine in new music," said Beth, with a little sigh, which no one heard but the hearth brush and kettle-holder.

"I shall get a nice box of Faber's drawing pencils; I really need them," said Amy decidedly.

"Mother didn't say anything about our money, and she won't wish us to give up everything. Let's each buy what we want, and have a little fun; I'm sure we work hard enough to earn it," cried Jo, examining the heels of her shoes in a gentlemanly manner.

"I know I do--teaching those tiresome children nearly all day, when I'm longing to enjoy myself at home," began Meg, in the complaining tone again.

"You don't have half such a hard time as I do," said Jo. "How would you like to be shut up for hours with a nervous, fussy old lady, who keeps you trotting, is never satisfied, and worries you till you're ready to fly out the window or cry?"

"It's naughty to fret, but I do think washing dishes and keeping things tidy is the worst work in the world. It makes me cross, and my hands get so stiff, I can't practice well at all." And Beth looked at her rough hands with a sigh that any one could hear that time.

"I don't believe any of you suffer as I do," cried Amy, "for you don't have to go to school with impertinent girls, who plague you if you don't know your lessons, and laugh at your dresses, and label your father if he isn't rich, and insult you when your nose isn't nice."

"If you mean libel, I'd say so, and not talk about labels, as if Papa was a pickle bottle," advised Jo, laughing.

"I know what I mean, and you needn't be statirical about it. It's proper to use good words, and improve your vocabilary," returned Amy, with dignity.

"Don't peck at one another, children. Don't you wish we had the money Papa lost when we were little, Jo? Dear me! How happy and good we'd be, if we had no worries!" said Meg, who could remember better times.

"You said the other day you thought we were a deal happier than the King children, for they were fighting and fretting all the time, in spite of their money."

"So I did, Beth. Well, I think we are. For though we do have to work, we make fun of ourselves, and are a pretty jolly set, as Jo would say."

"Jo does use such slang words!" observed Amy, with a reproving look at the long figure stretched on the rug.

Jo immediately sat up, put her hands in her pockets, and began to whistle.

"Don't, Jo. It's so boyish!"

"That's why I do it."

"I detest rude, unladylike girls!"

"I hate affected, niminy-piminy chits!"

"Birds in their little nests agree," sang Beth, the peacemaker, with such a funny face that both sharp voices softened to a laugh, and the "pecking" ended for that time.

"Really, girls, you are both to be blamed," said Meg, beginning to lecture in her elder-sisterly fashion. "You are old enough to leave off boyish tricks, and to behave better, Josephine. It didn't matter so much when you were a little girl, but now you are so tall, and turn up your hair, you should remember that you are a young lady."

"I'm not! And if turning up my hair makes me one, I'll wear it in two tails till I'm twenty," cried Jo, pulling off her net, and shaking down a chestnut mane. "I hate to think I've got to grow up, and be Miss March, and wear long gowns, and look as prim as a China Aster! It's bad enough to be a girl, anyway, when I like boy's games and work and manners! I can't get over my disappointment in not being a boy. And it's worse than ever now, for I'm dying to go and fight with Papa. And I can only stay home and knit, like a poky old woman!"

And Jo shook the blue army sock till the needles rattled like castanets, and her ball bounded across the room.

"Poor Jo! It's too bad, but it can't be helped. So you must try to be contented with making your name boyish, and playing brother to us girls," said Beth, stroking the rough head with a hand that all the dish washing and dusting in the world could not make ungentle in its touch.

"As for you, Amy," continued Meg, "you are altogether too particular and prim. Your airs are funny now, but you'll grow up an affected little goose, if you don't take care. I like your nice manners and refined ways of speaking, when you don't try to be elegant. But your absurd words are as bad as Jo's slang."

"If Jo is a tomboy and Amy a goose, what am I, please?" asked Beth, ready to share the lecture.

"You're a dear, and nothing else," answered Meg warmly, and no one contradicted her, for the 'Mouse' was the pet of the family.

As young readers like to know 'how people look', we will take this moment to give them a little sketch of the four sisters, who sat knitting away in the twilight, while the December snow fell quietly without, and the fire crackled cheerfully within. It was a comfortable room, though the carpet was faded and the furniture very plain, for a good picture or two hung on the walls, books filled the recesses, chrysanthemums and Christmas roses bloomed in the windows, and a pleasant atmosphere of home peace pervaded it.

Margaret, the eldest of the four, was sixteen, and very pretty, being plump and fair, with large eyes, plenty of soft brown hair, a sweet mouth, and white hands, of which she was rather vain. Fifteen-year-old Jo was very tall, thin, and brown, and reminded one of a colt, for she never seemed to know what to do with her long limbs, which were very much in her way. She had a decided mouth, a comical nose, and sharp, gray eyes, which appeared to see everything, and were by turns fierce, funny, or thoughtful. Her long, thick hair was her one beauty, but it was usually bundled into a net, to be out of her way. Round shoulders had Jo, big hands and feet, a flyaway look to her clothes, and the uncomfortable appearance of a girl who was rapidly shooting up into a woman and didn't like it. Elizabeth, or Beth, as everyone called her, was a rosy, smooth-haired, bright-eyed girl of thirteen, with a shy manner, a timid voice, and a peaceful expression which was seldom disturbed. Her father called her 'Little Miss Tranquility', and the name suited her excellently, for she seemed to live in a happy world of her own, only venturing out to meet the few whom she trusted and loved. Amy, though the youngest, was a most important person, in her own opinion at least. A regular snow maiden, with blue eyes, and yellow hair curling on her shoulders, pale and slender, and always carrying herself like a young lady mindful of her manners. What the characters of the four sisters were we will leave to be found out.

The clock struck six and, having swept up the hearth, Beth put a pair of slippers down to warm. Somehow the sight of the old shoes had a good effect upon the girls, for Mother was coming, and everyone brightened to welcome her. Meg stopped lecturing, and lighted the lamp, Amy got out of the easy chair without being asked, and Jo forgot how tired she was as she sat up to hold the slippers nearer to the blaze.

"They are quite worn out. Marmee must have a new pair."

"I thought I'd get her some with my dollar," said Beth.

"No, I shall!" cried Amy.

"I'm the oldest," began Meg, but Jo cut in with a decided, "I'm the man of the family now Papa is away, and I shall provide the slippers, for he told me to take special care of Mother while he was gone."

"I'll tell you what we'll do," said Beth, "let's each get her something for Christmas, and not get anything for ourselves."

"That's like you, dear! What will we get?" exclaimed Jo.

Everyone thought soberly for a minute, then Meg announced, as if the idea was suggested by the sight of her own pretty hands, "I shall give her a nice pair of gloves."

"Army shoes, best to be had," cried Jo.

"Some handkerchiefs, all hemmed," said Beth.

"I'll get a little bottle of cologne. She likes it, and it won't cost much, so I'll have some left to buy my pencils," added Amy.

"How will we give the things?" asked Meg.

"Put them on the table, and bring her in and see her open the bundles. Don't you remember how we used to do on our birthdays?" answered Jo.

"I used to be so frightened when it was my turn to sit in the chair with the crown on, and see you all come marching round to give the presents, with a kiss. I liked the things and the kisses, but it was dreadful to have you sit looking at me while I opened the bundles,"said Beth, who was toasting her face and the bread for tea at the same time.

"Let Marmee think we are getting things for ourselves, and then surprise her. We must go shopping tomorrow afternoon, Meg."

"Glad to find you so merry, my girls," said a cheery voice at the door, and all turned to welcome a tall, motherly lady with a 'can I help you' look about her which was truly delightful. She was not elegantly dressed, but a noble-looking woman, and the girls thought the gray cloak and unfashionable bonnet covered the most splendid mother in the world.

"Well, dearies, how have you got on today? There was so much to do, getting the boxes ready to go tomorrow, that I didn't come home to dinner. Has anyone called, Beth? How is your cold, Meg? Jo, you look tired to death. Come and kiss me, baby."

While making these maternal inquiries Mrs. March got her wet things off, her warm slippers on, and sitting down in the easy chair, drew Amy to her lap, preparing to enjoy the happiest hour of her busy day. The girls flew about, trying to make things comfortable, each in her own way. Meg arranged the tea table, Jo brought wood and set chairs, dropping, over-turning, and clattering everything she touched. Beth trotted to and fro between parlor kitchen, quiet and busy, while Amy gave directions to everyone, as she sat with her hands folded.

As they gathered about the table, Mrs. March said, with a particularly happy face, "I've got a treat for you after supper."

A quick, bright smile went round like a streak of sunshine. Beth clapped her hands, regardless of the biscuit she held, and Jo tossed up her napkin, crying, "A letter! A letter! Three cheers for Father!"

"Yes, a nice long letter. He is well, and thinks he shall get through the cold season better than we feared. He sends all sorts of loving wishes for Christmas, and an especial message to you girls," said Mrs. March, patting her pocket as if she had got a treasure there.

"Hurry and get done! Don't stop to quirk your little finger and simper over your plate, Amy," cried Jo, choking on her tea and dropping her bread, butter side down, on the carpet in her haste to get at the treat.

Beth ate no more, but crept away to sit in her shadowy corner and brood over the delight to come, till the others were ready.

"I think it was so splendid in Father to go as chaplain when he was too old to be drafted, and not strong enough for a soldier," said Meg warmly.

"Don't I wish I could go as a drummer, a vivan--what's its name? Or a nurse, so I could be near him and help him," exclaimed Jo, with a groan.

"It must be very disagreeable to sleep in a tent, and eat all sorts of bad-tasting things, and drink out of a tin mug," sighed Amy.

"When will he come home, Marmee?" asked Beth, with a little quiver in her voice.

"Not for many months, dear, unless he is sick. He will stay and do his work faithfully as long as he can, and we won't ask for him back a minute sooner than he can be spared. Now come and hear the letter."

They all drew to the fire, Mother in the big chair with Beth at her feet, Meg and Amy perched on either arm of the chair, and Jo leaning on the back, where no one would see any sign of emotion if the letter should happen to be touching. Very few letters were written in those hard times that were not touching, especially those which fathers sent home. In this one little was said of the hardships endured, the dangers faced, or the homesickness conquered. It was a cheerful, hopeful letter, full of lively descriptions of camp life, marches, and military news, and only at the end did the writer's heart over-flow with fatherly love and longing for the little girls at home.

"Give them all of my dear love and a kiss. Tell them I think of them by day, pray for them by night, and find my best comfort in their affection at all times. A year seems very long to wait before I see them, but remind them that while we wait we may all work, so that these hard days need not be wasted. I know they will remember all I said to them, that they will be loving children to you, will do their duty faithfully, fight their bosom enemies bravely, and conquer themselves so beautifully that when I come back to them I may be fonder and prouder than ever of my little women." Everybody sniffed when they came to that part. Jo wasn't ashamed of the great tear that dropped off the end of her nose, and Amy never minded the rumpling of her curls as she hid her face on her mother's shoulder and sobbed out, "I am a selfish girl! But I'll truly try to be better, so he mayn't be disappointed in me by-and-by."

"We all will," cried Meg. "I think too much of my looks and hate to work, but won't any more, if I can help it."

"I'll try and be what he loves to call me, 'a little woman' and not be rough and wild, but do my duty here instead of wanting to be somewhere else," said Jo, thinking that keeping her temper at home was a much harder task than facing a rebel or two down South.

Beth said nothing, but wiped away her tears with the blue army sock and began to knit with all her might, losing no time in doing the duty that lay nearest her, while she resolved in her quiet little soul to be all that Father hoped to find her when the year brought round the happy coming home.

Mrs. March broke the silence that followed Jo's words, by saying in her cheery voice, "Do you remember how you used to play Pilgrims Progress when you were little things? Nothing delighted you more than to have me tie my piece bags on your backs for burdens, give you hats and sticks and rolls of paper, and let you travel through the house from the cellar, which was the City of Destruction, up, up, to the housetop, where you had all the lovely things you could collect to make a Celestial City."

"What fun it was, especially going by the lions, fighting Apollyon, and passing through the valley where the hob-goblins were," said Jo.

"I liked the place where the bundles fell off and tumbled downstairs," said Meg.

"I don't remember much about it, except that I was afraid of the cellar and the dark entry, and always liked the cake and milk we had up at the top. If I wasn't too old for such things, I'd rather like to play it over again," said Amy, who began to talk of renouncing childish things at the mature age of twelve.

"We never are too old for this, my dear, because it is a play we are playing all the time in one way or another. Our burdens are here, our road is before us, and the longing for goodness and happiness is the guide that leads us through many troubles and mistakes to the peace which is a true Celestial City. Now, my little pilgrims, suppose you begin again, not in play, but in earnest, and see how far on you can get before Father comes home."

"Really, Mother? Where are our bundles?" asked Amy, who was a very literal young lady.

"Each of you told what your burden was just now, except Beth. I rather think she hasn't got any," said her mother.

"Yes, I have. Mine is dishes and dusters, and envying girls with nice pianos, and being afraid of people."

Beth's bundle was such a funny one that everybody wanted to laugh, but nobody did, for it would have hurt her feelings very much.

"Let us do it," said Meg thoughtfully. "It is only another name for trying to be good, and the story may help us, for though we do want to be good, it's hard work and we forget, and don't do our best."

"We were in the Slough of Despond tonight, and Mother came and pulled us out as Help did in the book. We ought to have our roll of directions, like Christian. What shall we do about that?" asked Jo, delighted with the fancy which lent a little romance to the very dull task of doing her duty.

"Look under your pillows Christmas morning, and you will find your guidebook," replied Mrs. March.

They talked over the new plan while old Hannah cleared the table, then out came the four little work baskets, and the needles flew as the girls made sheets for Aunt March. It was uninteresting sewing, but tonight no one grumbled. They adopted Jo's plan of dividing the long seams into four parts, and calling the quarters Europe, Asia, Africa, and America, and in that way got on capitally, especially when they talked about the different countries as they stitched their way through them.

At nine they stopped work, and sang, as usual, before they went to bed.

No one but Beth could get much music out of the old piano, but she had a way of softly touching the yellow keys and making a pleasant accompaniment to the simple songs they sang. Meg had a voice like a flute, and she and her mother led the little choir. Amy chirped like a cricket, and Jo wandered through the airs at her own sweet will, always coming out at the wrong place with a croak or a quaver that spoiled the most pensive tune. They had always done this from the time they could lisp...

"Crinkle, crinkle, 'ittle 'tar,"

and it had become a household custom, for the mother was a born singer. The first sound in the morning was her voice as she went about the house singing like a lark, and the last sound at night was the same cheery sound, for the girls never grew too old for that familiar lullaby.

Jo was the first to wake in the gray dawn of Christmas morning. No stockings hung at the fireplace, and for a moment she felt as much disappointed as she did long ago, when her little sock fell down because it was crammed so full of goodies. Then she remembered her mother's promise and, slipping her hand under her pillow, drew out a little crimson-covered book. She knew it very well, for it was that beautiful old story of the best life ever lived, and Jo felt that it was a true guidebook for any pilgrim going on a long journey. She woke Meg with a "Merry Christmas," and bade her see what was under her pillow. A green-covered book appeared, with the same picture inside, and a few words written by their mother, which made their one present very precious in their eyes. Presently Beth and Amy woke to rummage and find their little books also, one dove-colored, the other blue, and all sat looking at and talking about them, while the east grew rosy with the coming day.

In spite of her small vanities, Margaret had a sweet and pious nature, which unconsciously influenced her sisters, especially Jo, who loved her very tenderly, and obeyed her because her advice was so gently given.

"Girls," said Meg seriously, looking from the tumbled head beside her to the two little night-capped ones in the room beyond, "Mother wants us to read and love and mind these books, and we must begin at once. We used to be faithful about it, but since Father went away and all this war trouble unsettled us, we have neglected many things. You can do as you please, but I shall keep my book on the table here and read a little every morning as soon as I wake, for I know it will do me good and help me through the day."

Then she opened her new book and began to read. Jo put her arm round her and, leaning cheek to cheek, read also, with the quiet expression so seldom seen on her restless face.

"How good Meg is! Come, Amy, let's do as they do. I'll help you with the hard words, and they'll explain things if we don't understand," whispered Beth, very much impressed by the pretty books and her sisters' example.

"I'm glad mine is blue," said Amy. And then the rooms were very still while the pages were softly turned, and the winter sunshine crept in to touch the bright heads and serious faces with a Christmas greeting.

"Where is Mother?" asked Meg, as she and Jo ran down to thank her for their gifts, half an hour later.

"Goodness only knows. Some poor creeter came a-beggin', and your ma went straight off to see what was needed. There never was such a woman for givin' away vittles and drink, clothes and firin'," replied Hannah, who had lived with the family since Meg was born, and was considered by them all more as a friend than a servant.

"She will be back soon, I think, so fry your cakes, and have everything ready," said Meg, looking over the presents which were collected in a basket and kept under the sofa, ready to be produced at the proper time. "Why, where is Amy's bottle of cologne?" she added, as the little flask did not appear.

"She took it out a minute ago, and went off with it to put a ribbon on it, or some such notion," replied Jo, dancing about the room to take the first stiffness off the new army slippers.

"How nice my handkerchiefs look, don't they? Hannah washed and ironed them for me, and I marked them all myself," said Beth, looking proudly at the somewhat uneven letters which had cost her such labor.

"Bless the child! She's gone and put 'Mother' on them instead of 'M. March'. How funny!" cried Jo, taking one up.

"Isn't that right? I thought it was better to do it so, because Meg's initials are M.M., and I don't want anyone to use these but Marmee," said Beth, looking troubled.

"It's all right, dear, and a very pretty idea, quite sensible too, for no one can ever mistake now. It will please her very much, I know," said Meg, with a frown for Jo and a smile for Beth.

"There's Mother. Hide the basket, quick!" cried Jo, as a door slammed and steps sounded in the hall.

Amy came in hastily, and looked rather abashed when she saw her sisters all waiting for her.

"Where have you been, and what are you hiding behind you?" asked Meg, surprised to see, by her hood and cloak, that lazy Amy had been out so early.

"Don't laugh at me, Jo! I didn't mean anyone should know till the time came. I only meant to change the little bottle for a big one, and I gave all my money to get it, and I'm truly trying not to be selfish any more."

As she spoke, Amy showed the handsome flask which replaced the cheap one, and looked so earnest and humble in her little effort to forget herself that Meg hugged her on the spot, and Jo pronounced her 'a trump', while Beth ran to the window, and picked her finest rose to ornament the stately bottle.

"You see I felt ashamed of my present, after reading and talking about being good this morning, so I ran round the corner and changed it the minute I was up, and I'm so glad, for mine is the handsomest now."

Another bang of the street door sent the basket under the sofa, and the girls to the table, eager for breakfast.

"Merry Christmas, Marmee! Many of them! Thank you for our books. We read some, and mean to every day," they all cried in chorus.

"Merry Christmas, little daughters! I'm glad you began at once, and hope you will keep on. But I want to say one word before we sit down. Not far away from here lies a poor woman with a little newborn baby. Six children are huddled into one bed to keep from freezing, for they have no fire. There is nothing to eat over there, and the oldest boy came to tell me they were suffering hunger and cold. My girls, will you give them your breakfast as a Christmas present?"

They were all unusually hungry, having waited nearly an hour, and for a minute no one spoke, only a minute, for Jo exclaimed impetuously, "I'm so glad you came before we began!"

"May I go and help carry the things to the poor little children?" asked Beth eagerly.

"I shall take the cream and the muffings," added Amy, heroically giving up the article she most liked.

Meg was already covering the buckwheats, and piling the bread into one big plate.

"I thought you'd do it," said Mrs. March, smiling as if satisfied. "You shall all go and help me, and when we come back we will have bread and milk for breakfast, and make it up at dinnertime."

They were soon ready, and the procession set out. Fortunately it was early, and they went through back streets, so few people saw them, and no one laughed at the queer party.

A poor, bare, miserable room it was, with broken windows, no fire, ragged bedclothes, a sick mother, wailing baby, and a group of pale, hungry children cuddled under one old quilt, trying to keep warm.

How the big eyes stared and the blue lips smiled as the girls went in.

"Ach, mein Gott! It is good angels come to us!" said the poor woman, crying for joy.

"Funny angels in hoods and mittens," said Jo, and set them to laughing.

In a few minutes it really did seem as if kind spirits had been at work there. Hannah, who had carried wood, made a fire, and stopped up the broken panes with old hats and her own cloak. Mrs. March gave the mother tea and gruel, and comforted her with promises of help, while she dressed the little baby as tenderly as if it had been her own.

The girls meantime spread the table, set the children round the fire, and fed them like so many hungry birds, laughing, talking, and trying to understand the funny broken English.

"Das ist gut!" "Die Engel-kinder!" cried the poor things as they ate and warmed their purple hands at the comfortable blaze. The girls had never been called angel children before, and thought it very agreeable, especially Jo, who had been considered a 'Sancho' ever since she was born. That was a very happy breakfast, though they didn't get any of it. And when they went away, leaving comfort behind, I think there were not in all the city four merrier people than the hungry little girls who gave away their breakfasts and contented themselves with bread and milk on Christmas morning.

"That's loving our neighbor better than ourselves, and I like it," said Meg, as they set out their presents while their mother was upstairs collecting clothes for the poor Hummels.

Not a very splendid show, but there was a great deal of love done up in the few little bundles, and the tall vase of red roses, white chrysanthemums, and trailing vines, which stood in the middle, gave quite an elegant air to the table.

"She's coming! Strike up, Beth! Open the door, Amy! Three cheers for Marmee!" cried Jo, prancing about while Meg went to conduct Mother to the seat of honor.

Beth played her gayest march, Amy threw open the door, and Meg enacted escort with great dignity. Mrs. March was both surprised and touched, and smiled with her eyes full as she examined her presents and read the little notes which accompanied them. The slippers went on at once, a new handkerchief was slipped into her pocket, well scented with Amy's cologne, the rose was fastened in her bosom, and the nice gloves were pronounced a perfect fit.

There was a good deal of laughing and kissing and explaining, in the simple, loving fashion which makes these home festivals so pleasant at the time, so sweet to remember long afterward, and then all fell to work.

(Later that evening... after a play had been enacted by the girls....)

The excitement had hardly subsided when Hannah appeared, with, "Mrs. March's compliments, and would the ladies walk down to supper."

This was a surprise even to the actors, and when they saw the table, they looked at one another in rapturous amazement. It was like Marmee to get up a little treat for them, but anything so fine as this was unheard of since the departed days of plenty. There was ice cream, actually two dishes of it, pink and white, and cake and fruit and distracting French bonbons and, in the middle of the table, four great bouquets of hot house flowers.

It quite took their breath away, and they stared first at the table and then at their mother, who looked as if she enjoyed it immensely.

"Is it fairies?" asked Amy.

"Santa Claus," said Beth.

"Mother did it." And Meg smiled her sweetest.

"Aunt March had a good fit and sent the supper," cried Jo, with a sudden inspiration.

"All wrong. Old Mr. Laurence sent it," replied Mrs. March.

"The Laurence boy's grandfather! What in the world put such a thing into his head? We don't know him!" exclaimed Meg.

"Hannah told one of his servants about your breakfast party. He is an odd old gentleman, but that pleased him. He knew my father years ago, and he sent me a polite note this afternoon, saying he hoped I would allow him to express his friendly feeling toward my children by sending them a few trifles in honor of the day. I could not refuse, and so you have a little feast at night to make up for the bread-and-milk breakfast."

So as the plates went round, and the ice began to melt out of sight, with ohs and ahs of satisfaction.

"I never had such a fine bouquet before! How pretty it is!" And Meg examined her flowers with great interest.

"They are lovely. But Beth's roses are sweeter to me," said Mrs. March, smelling the half-dead posy in her belt.

Beth nestled up to her, and whispered softly, "I wish I could send my bunch to Father. I'm afraid he isn't having such a merry Christmas as we are."

A Christmas Story...
by A Nun of Grace.

..for children, and the young of heart of all ages.

The Christmas-Tree Angel sneezed, opened her eyes, wished she hadn't - and sneezed again...

All she could see was the moth-eaten, ragged remains of something old and woolly, and very dirty and dusty.

Oh, but not quite all!

That was what had awoken her.

That glimmering shimmer of starlight which somehow had worked through her dismal coverings.

It could only be the Christmas Star - winning through the rags and the grimy skylight...

Christmas!

The Angel struggled to sit up, using her grimy elbows to poke through the smothering rags…

Christmas!

Oh, joy of joys!

Her heart, deep in her cloth breast, swelled and soared...

But where was she?

It must be the attic.

Yes.

But when she had last been put away, the children's loving hands regretful, their mother gently reassuring them that soon, soon, Christmas would come again, all had been neat and clean and orderly.

Now?

Chaos, dirt, disorder...rusty old grates, mouldy old clothes...

And what had happened to her sparkling white dress?

All tattered and filthy…

And her wings!

Oh her poor wings!

All broken...

A tear came to her eye.

And suddenly she heard, oh, sweet sound.

Carols, children's voices, far, far below.

That, too was what had woken her from a long, long sleep.

And the surge of love woke again in her sore heart.

Love is magic; and strong magic indeed on a Holy Night.

For as the Angel had realised, this was indeed that Holiest of all nights.
The Eve of the Nativity.

When God-in-Christ- so- small came among us...

And she looked down.

And the floors became as glass.

And she could see all the big, tall house where she had flown at the top of tall, fragrant Christmas trees, a new, sparkly dress every year, for many generations.

All the storeys, and all the rooms, all.

And she realised that she was not in the old attic.

There all had been clean and neat and orderly.

No; she had been thrust, seemingly with a lot of rubbish, into a loft above the attic.

Now, through the floor that had become as glass, she saw the real attic.

And what she saw made her shiver.

She wrapped a fold of the dirty wool round her bare shoulders, and gazed down.

A young man sat there, in collar and tie and smart trousers, before a large computer screen full of figures and formulas.

The room was bare of any tree, or card, or even a sprig of holly.

Nothing to show that this was the Holy Night.

Bare too of colour and life.

All was glass and chrome, grey and black and white.

The Angel's heart swelled with compassion.

And she peered into his tiny kitchen, so immaculately and unnaturally clean – and so bare and impersonal.

The fridge and cupboards contained not so much as a mince pie or a chicken leg.

Skimmed milk!

Decaffeinated coffee!

Organic cottage cheese!

Broccoli sprigs!

She shook her tattered head, and her halo fell over one eye...

HER children were always full of Christmas!

Of JOY and LIFE.

And their Christmasses celebrated the Coming of Jesus joyously, with feasting and rejoicing.

This poor young man!

A tear fell from her eye - and landed on the young man's head.

Startled, he put his hand up, and wiped the crystal moisture away.

And for a moment his studious, serious face softened - and the carolling grew louder...

Just for a moment the Love broke through.

But the computer bleeped its soulless music and the magic was broken...

And he resumed his gazing and tapping.

The Light was gone from his face.

And the sound of holy singing died away...

And the Angel's eyes were drawn downwards, to the next floor of the rambling old house…

And, oh, such a different scene!

The carols rang loud and sweet and true now!!

There was colour and light; that was her first impression.

A fire burned, and by the hearth, a young mother sat, a baby asleep in her arms, as she watched her children, lovelight in her eyes.

A boy of about six, curly-headed and sturdy, sat, engrossed in colouring cards, at the table.

A younger girl, about three, her hair white-blonde, played with the figures of a Crib, her face animated, her lips moving as she fingered the familiar figures.

A Christmas tree twinkled and glowed joyously in a corner.

And there were bright cards and lovingly- made paper garlands everywhere.

And three stockings hung from the mantlepiece.

The little girl ran to her mother.

"I'm cold, Mummy!"

And as the young mother wrapped her arms of love around her child, the music hesitated, and the Angel saw more clearly.

The fire skulked low and mean in the night chill.

The children were too thinly clad for the winter- time, sleeves too short.

The tree was a tattered old artificial one...

The furniture was shabby and down-at- heel.

With compassion surging, the Angel sought out the kitchen.

Cold, cold, cold.

The tiniest chicken she had ever seen waited in the oven; all legs and bones.

A large pan of potatoes, and carrots enough.

And a small Christmas pudding.

For all these folk?

She saw now how thin the mother was; dark rings under worried eyes.

No father here then.

And no work with a young baby...

But the love radiating!

The shining of it!

Jenny sent Benjamin, who had also come to her, for the bread.

Making toast on the glowing embers was a warming and absorbing task!

So they gathered in the fireglow...

The Light in their hearts and on their faces.

And Jenny fed her babe, an ache in her heart.

Jeff had died too suddenly and too unexpectedly to have made provision for his young family.

And he had been struggling to set up in business, a calculatedly lean time for them.

So it was a struggle now, with the new baby too..

Sighing, the Angel looked down, as the threadbare rug on the cold lino became as glass.

And she blinked at what she saw!

Opulence, luxury!

A big log-effect electric fire blazed in the hearth, and radiators pulsed heat.

Rich, thick carpets, deep soft armchairs, and the sheen of highly polished wood.

A huge tree, redolent of pine, and shining and shimmering with long-piled tinsel and glass ornaments.

Fruit in crystal bowls; expensive chocolates...

And by the fire...

One small person?

An old lady, a glass in her hand, expensively dressed and coiffeured...

But where was the happiness?

The carols were silent now, for there was not here that love they needed to sing in…

Her face held no happiness.

No Light here.

The Angel looked in the kitchen.

Oh, so warm and fitted with all manner of devices.

And the large fridge groaning and packed.

Cheeses of every nation,

Cream.

Pate and sausage…

Ham...

And a small but plump turkey nestling, well-stuffed, among tiny sausages and bacon rolls…

And desserts!

Ice-cream…

Cream filled eclairs jostled and elbowed each other in the freezer...

A large, elaborately iced cake…

Tins of shortbread and chocolate biscuits...

The Angel fairly bristled with indignation!

There were those little cherub-mites, a few feet above all this rich indulgence, making toast with the cheapest bread, on a tiny fire!

Cuddling together for warmth...

And that young man!

Ignorant and insouciant, lost in his tiny, unreal electronic world...

She frowned, an idea birthing in her...

And as she pondered, the compassion radiated and spread out from her in that love that is itself the strongest prayer there is.

Selfless and reaching out...

Her heart almost burst with that love.

And outside, unforecast, unheralded by mortal meteorologists, snow began falling.

Christmas snow, thick, soft, veiling the human harshness of the world,

Cloaking all with the silence and purity of Heaven.

Large shining flakes, dancing in Heaven's ageless rhythms...

And the carols soared and gathered power.

Why, the very angels sang with them.

Voices sweet and pure and holy...

The saints in heaven gathered, singing, carolling, and watched, breath bated, prayer a tangible incense now...

All focused on this tall house and its people...

For God is a God who loves each soul as the good Father He is...

And the Angel, love strong in her cloth breast, hurt for the hurt, cold for the cold, grieving for the grieving, shuddered with adoration and longing.

And the snow fell heavy, heavy, heavy...

And the power lines sagged, sagged, sagged.

The young mother, her three children gathered around her, folded under her blue shawl like chicks under a hen's wings, gazed into the embers of the fire...

The young man stretched and yawned, thinking of his bed...

The old lady sipped her drink and closed her eyes...

And with a silent exultation, as silent as the Birth that night, the world man had made went suddenly dark…

As the power lines refused to accept the weight of the thick, thick snow.

No street lights...

Only the Christmas starlight, the huge, lambent winter moon.

And that one, huge, radiant star...

Outshining all the rest...

The mother and her children did not even notice that the power had gone.

They were engrossed in toast and love!

Warm together by the firelight and candle-light, safe in their loving ...

The young man was terrified!

His whole world, in his close-curtained attic, suddenly went black.

Then he realised, through his panic, that it was a power cut.

He had never thought to buy candles or a torch.

So he groped his slow, clumsy way across to the window.

Loud agony as he stubbed his toes on the inimical, angular edges of his cold, metal furniture.

And the sight when he pulled the thick curtains aside took his unwary breath away.

A white, bright world...

No lights made by man.

Starlight.

Silence.

And that huge, huge smiling moon over the pure, still world.

He stood, mesmerised...

The old lady was startled beyond measure.

Suddenly her luxurious nest was dark.

And it began to grow very cold amazingly quickly...

She shivered in her fashionably thin clothes...

She thought longingly of bed - but the electric blanket would not be on, and fine linen sheets are very cold...

All her home was electric.

Not so much as a gas ring...

Not a candle to be had...

Memories of a long -ago childhood began to steal into her mind.

A poor home - and a poverty she had vowed never to be near again.

But there had been warmth of a different kind, she realised, with a sudden pang...

Too many children, too few clothes, too little food, and that poor.

But, oh the love!

Tears pricked at her lonely eyes –

And suddenly she heard a baby cry...

And, for the first time, she thought of the young family upstairs.

She, being on the ground floor, and with her own entrance, had found it easy to avoid contact.

She had no idea how they lived, frowned at childish noise...

But how would they cope?

The young man heard that thin wail too.

He also had avoided contact with the other residents.

Sometimes, inevitably, they met on the stairs, but he rushed past, always in a hurry to get to his computer..

But also, and he knew this now with a painful clarity, because in the Children's Home he had been brought up in, there had been too many kids, far too many, and too little affection.

Always someone else needing and getting attention, until he gave up seeking any.

He lost himself first in books, then in his electronic world, at work and at home...

Suddenly, the light of that bright Star entered his soul...

At the same time as it did the old lady's...

Oh the power of helplessness!

The strength of the thin cry of a tiny baby!

The old lady and the young man met at the door of the flat where the young family were wrapped and enfolded in warmth.

The moon beamed in on them, its silvery light ghostly and unreal.

They looked sheepishly at each other - and started talking at the same time...

"I just wondered..."

"The baby..."

And the young mother heard them, and opened the door hesitantly.

The baby was held in her blue-shawled arms.

The candlelight flickered around her with the sudden movement of air.

The two neighbours gasped.

For Love at Christmas is tangible...

Especially where a mother and baby are...

Here were they, cold and dark on the landing, their rich homes dark and empty.

And here were these, in a warm, light sanctuary...

Jenny, of course, solicitous, invited them in as soon as she heard about the power cut.

Love is mother to all.

She shooed them gently to the fire.

And set the kettle to boil on the old gas cooker for a pot of hot tea…

And set Benjamin to making more toast.

She opened the precious pot of honey she had been saving…

And put more scarce coal on the fire…

Lit more candles…

For every stranger in need is the Christ-Child.

Becky, her mother's daughter, once her short shyness had worn off, snuggled up to Miss Marsh.

That contact with the physical warmth of the loving, unjudging child took the old lady's breath away...

And Benjamin showed his craft work to Colin...

And engrossed him in the intricacies; a sharing that was full and whole.

And the young man's lonely heart began to mend.

And the carols soared outside.

And no-one thought to wonder who was out there in the thick, thick snow.

For Christmas magic was too strong now for human minds to question.

And they all, replete and warm, joined in...

Becky by now was snuggled on Miss Marsh's unaccustomed lap.

Benjamin and Colin, the boy and young man side by side on the settee...

Miss Marsh and Colin were spellbound...

But could not help but notice how worn and thin all was.

How little this loving and generous family had...

And Miss Marsh found herself thinking about her home.

Of all she had ready there.
Of the rich, abundant food...

She cleared her throat nervously - for she realised that this poor family was rich in ways she could never aspire to, and needed not her bounty...

"I was wondering... how would you like to come to me tomorrow? For Christmas dinner, I mean? All of you?"

And she smiled at Colin also.

There was silence...

The very carols paused in mid-verse...

Becky broke the awkwardness she in her child-likeness had no awareness of.

In her simplicity there were no overtones, no subtlety of undercurrents...

"PLEASE, Mummy! I love Miss Marsh!"

Jenny's gaze was keen. If this was charity...

But the carols started again, and she saw with sudden clarity the lonely lines on the old face... and the lostness in the young man's eyes...

And she smiled.

A Christmas smile…

She had so little to give - but she had all.

So much love in these small, giant souls!

"Oh, that would be lovely! But you have no electricity! And it will be so cold down there. And who knows when the power will be back on?"

Miss Marsh knew a keen, sharp pang of pain and disappointment.

Then Colin, to whom the idea of Christmas had set off a train of longing, cleared his throat and spoke.

"Well, this is just an idea - and I have no Christmas stuff in, but if Jenny will agree, can we not - pool resources?"

Miss Marsh's face cleared, relief dancing through her.

"Yes of course! If Jenny will agree, I can bring all the food here. And we can cook it together?"

So that is what they did.

Miss Marsh and Colin went home clutching hot water bottles.

And in the snow-cold of that Christmas Day, they met to go to Church - for Jenny insisted they share all...

And each heart was thankful.

The snow had stopped, and the sun dazzled and radiated prisms and rainbows off the piled banks and ripples of it.

All the men had turned out with spades and shovels to clear paths on the pavements.

Colin had worked with them and his face shone with the air and exertion

There was still no power, but the Church was bright.

The sun glowed and rainbowed through the stained glass.

And darker corners were alive with candles.

For all who came brought them.
Small lights to make a great Light.

And all shared and smiled with a joyous camaraderie...

And the children, flanked by the adults, gathered round the Crib.

They celebrated the Coming of Jesus with whole hearts and strong voices.

And then a procession! The turkey was already sizzling in Jenny's oven.

And now they carried all the good things down, until the old table fairly groaned.

The children's faces were a picture!

Colin vanished, to return with a whole sack of coal, and bags of logs; an enterprising shop had opened its doors. ..

Boxes of candles.

And a bright jigsaw...

And the flat rang with laughter.

Delicious, rich aromas rose to heaven...

The Christmas-Tree Angel yawned and drooped.

Her mission accomplished, she was exhausted.

And as the winter afternoon early darkened into evening, she knew that her time was ending...

Indeed, she had had an extension, for Christmas-Tree Angels only come to life on Christmas Eve...

She gazed with love on the people below her, drinking in the glad faces, replete with more than good food...

Colin, working with Benjamin on the jigsaw...

Jenny nursing baby Jeff, his small face upturned to her.

Miss Marsh sharing the Crib with Becky...

The candles casting their soft light.

The logs blazing their living warmth.

Oh, it was so good; all so good!

And it was a love that would last, and grow and heal its givers and receivers...

Then, she started to feel...different

Instead of fading, she was coming to life in a new way...

She blinked...

And as she watched, her tattered, torn, dirty old dress began to change..

White, long, radiant…

Clean, pure...

And her shoulders began to prickle...

And her head felt different...
And the dirty skylight cleared, seemed to open...

Wide onto the starry heavens...

And the light from that bright star grew and radiated outwards.

Wider and wider

And brighter and brighter.

Until it encompassed and embraced all, all, all...

And oh!

The Christmas-Tree Angel...wide new, feathered wings outspread.

White gown flowing.

Bright-haloed head.

She floated and flew out, up.

The newest angel in God's Heaven...

To be where there is no rust or moth.

No cold or darkness...

No pain or sorrow.

Just pure Light.

Shining out from the Christ Child.

To all and through all who love Him.

Radiating out into the whole world.

Light and love and peace…

Jesus. Light of the World. ….Way, Truth, Life…

Replete, and sated with stories, her heart light and bright, Sister smoored the fire, carefully blew out the candles, and, the cats following step by step, for all the world like the page boy in "Good King Wenceslas"...

Up the wooden stairs, the fragrance of candles curling up beside them, to dream of Christmas under the skylight where the stars shone down.

With the promise of the One Star...the Morning Star, to warm and comfort.

The Fourth Verse...

Angels and Archangels
May have gathered there,
Cherubim and Seraphim
Thronged the air.

But His mother only,
In her maiden bliss,

Worshipped the Almighty,
With a kiss.

Light of the World....

The cottage lay silent under the Christmas Star.

Quiet, quiescent in the soft darkness.

The day had dawned clear and sharp with frost silvering all, stars sparkling rainbows. Daylight was slow to come and heralded by the aching sweetness of wren-carol and robin-song.

Then clouds had veiled the sharpness, softening with a tinge of grey and yellow.

And bringing early darkness.

Sister gazed into the heart of the turf fire, which tonight was crowned by a sturdy log she had set aside for this night, in an ancient tradition.

It fragranced the air gently, sharp and sweet. Slowly melting in the flames, giving as it was consumed of its very heart.

At midnight, the tall Christ-Candle would be lit.

But for now, peace and stillness.

The last of the Carols from Kings, heard through the computer as there was no radio signal there, had faded away, the lessons heard.

The day had brought welcome surprises. Two from the village had called, bearing gifts of seasonal food.

As if someone had told them of the feeding crisis overseas, and that, like all her Sisters, she had sent every cent she could, including what would have been spent on Christmas food.

It was no great worry; the Sisters sat lightly on such matters, and there was always food in the house.

But it was warmth and comfort to see such loving provision. So now, through the thoughtfulness and kindness of others, rushing round on Christmas Eve, festive fare abounded, with even a small turkey.

Sister had pondered on going down to Midnight Mass.

But then, before the Carols had begun, the lowering skies had released the first soft snowflakes.

And by darkfall, the pure beauty of a white veil lay over all, intensifying the hushed holiness.

So, in utter tranquility, Sister was effectively, high on her mountain, cut off from the outside world. Set apart in the hermitage.

And the words and songs of comfort echoed dreamily in her mind as she sat, her hands still for once, by firelight and candlelight, watching the red candle that burnt bright in the window, to guide Mary and Joseph, or any wandering soul, home to shelter and sanctuary.

Let all mortal flesh keep silence,
And with fear and trembling stand;
Ponder nothing earthly minded,
For with blessing in His hand,
Christ our God to earth descendeth,
Our full homage to demand.

King of kings, yet born of Mary,
As of old on earth He stood,
Lord of lords, in human vesture,
In the body and the blood;
He will give to all the faithful
His own self for heavenly food.

Rank on rank the host of heaven
Spreads its vanguard on the way,
As the Light of light descendeth
From the realms of endless day,
That the powers of hell may vanish
As the darkness clears away.

At His feet the six wingèd seraph,
Cherubim with sleepless eye,
Veil their faces to the presence,
As with ceaseless voice they cry:
Alleluia, Alleluia
Alleluia, Lord Most High!

"Now the birth of Jesus Christ was on this wise: When His mother Mary had been betrothed to Joseph, before they came together she was found with child of the Holy Ghost. And Joseph her husband, being a righteous man, and not willing to make her a public example, was minded to put her away privily. But when he thought on these things, behold, an angel of the Lord appeared unto him in a dream, saying, Joseph, thou son of David, fear not to take unto thee Mary thy wife: for that which is conceived in her is of the Holy Ghost. And she shall bring forth a Son; and thou shalt call His name Jesus;

for it is He that shall save His people from their sins. Now all this is come to pass, that it might be fulfilled which was spoken by the Lord through the prophet, saying,

> Behold, the virgin shall be with child and shall bring forth a Son, and they shall call His name Immanuel;

"Which is, being interpreted, God with us. And Joseph arose from his sleep, and did as the angel of the Lord commanded him, and took unto him his wife; and knew her not till she had brought forth a Son; and he called His name Jesus."

(Matthew i. 18-25.)

"And there were shepherds in the same country abiding in the field, and keeping watch by night over their flock. And an angel of the Lord stood by them, and the glory of the Lord shone round about them: and they were sore afraid. And the angel said unto them, Be not afraid; for behold, I bring you good tidings of great joy which shall be to all the people: for there is born to you this day in the city of David a Saviour, which is Christ the Lord.

"And this is the sign unto you; Ye shall find a babe wrapped in swaddling clothes, and lying in a manger. And suddenly there was with the angel a multitude of the heavenly host praising God, and saying,

> Glory to God in the highest,
> And on earth peace among men
> in whom He is well pleased.

"And it came to pass, when the angels went away from them into heaven, the shepherds said one to another, Let us now go even unto Bethlehem, and see this thing that is come to pass, which the Lord hath made known unto us. And they came with haste, and found both Mary and Joseph, and the Babe lying in the manger. And when they saw it, they made known concerning the saying which was spoken to them about this child.

"And all that heard it wondered at the things which were spoken unto them by the shepherds. But Mary kept all these sayings, pondering them in her heart. And the shepherds returned, glorifying and praising God for all the things that they had heard and seen, even as it was spoken unto them."

(Luke ii. 8-20.)

See amid the winter's snow,
Born for us on earth below,
See, the gentle Lamb appears,
Promised from eternal years.

Hail that ever blessèd morn,
Hail redemption's happy dawn,
Sing through all Jerusalem:
Christ is born in Bethlehem.

Lo, within a manger lies
He Who built the starry skies;

He Who, thronèd in height sublime,
Sits amid the cherubim.

Say, you holy shepherds, say,
Tell your joyful news today.
Why have you now left your sheep
On the lonely mountain steep?

"As we watched at dead of night,
Lo, we saw a wondrous light;
Angels singing 'Peace on earth'
Told us of the Savior's birth."

Sacred Infant, all divine,
What a tender love was Thine,
Thus to come from highest bliss
Down to such a world as this.
Teach, O teach us, holy Child,
By Thy face so meek and mild,
Teach us to resemble Thee,
In Thy sweet humility.

Christus Natus Est.....

ALLELUJAH.....

"In the beginning was the Word, and the Word was with God, and the Word was God. The same was in the beginning with God. All things were made by Him; and without Him was nothing made that was made. In Him was Life; and the Life was the Light of men. And the Light shineth in darkness; and the darkness comprehendeth it not.

There was a man sent from God, whose name was John. The same came for a witness, to bear witness of the Light, that all men might believe. He was not that Light, but came to bear witness of that Light. That was the true Light, which lighteth every man that cometh into the world. He was in the world, and the world was made by Him, and the world knew Him not. He came unto His own, and His own received Him not. But as many as received Him, to them gave He power to become the sons of God, even to them that believe in His Name. Which were born, not of blood, nor of the will of the flesh, nor of the will of man, but of God. And the Word was made flesh and dwelt among us, and we beheld His glory, the glory as of the only begotten of the Father, full of grace and truth."

John Chapter One

ALLELUIA!

AMEN…

ALLELUIA!

AMEN…

ALLELUIA!

AMEN!

Epilogue…

And so the year passes, and the years pass.

For Sister-on-the- mountain, and all her Sisters, wherever and however they live this life, the sweetness of hands busy, giving skills lent to them, and passing then that bright torch of loving and surrendering on.

Seasons and years…

Old Nun, in springtime sun...
Her music the birds' sweet orison…
Fingers flying through fine cream
wool...

A shawl for a baby she will never see,
Far away across the sea…

Old Nun in summer rain,
Watching the streaming window pane,
Hands working a rainbow of mitts,
For winter- children she will never see,
Far away across the sea…

Old Nun in autumn gales,
Seeing the green world fade and pale,
Lap heaped high with thick warm hats,
For old and cold she will never meet,
Far away across the sea…

Old Nun in winter snow -
Homeward-bound.. not far to go.
Winding white wool...slow, pensive hands,
Rapt in the dove-wings heavenly dance…

To be worked by Sisters she will never see…
Far away across the sea…

Seasons of soul, seasons of heart,
Seasons together, seasons apart…
Rain and snow, wind and rain…
Mattering nothing, the ache or the pain...

Always the Son, always that gain
Of love given freely, of life fully shared,
Of heaven on earth, of Jesus in heart.

Always the love, that bright, strongwrought thread…
Enfolding, embracing, a healing of heaven.

Many times are we asked, how we began, who was our Foundress, the where, the when… the why.

Many times there has been the intention to write all these things and more, but always there are other things.

For hungry children come before all else.

And when the Order almost died out a score or more years ago, all the records were left in a damp cellar in England.

They were, in that sad state, taken to Canada when the Mother House moved there, and when our Convent there was washed away by floods, once more they were saturated.

The task of trying to salvage is a time -consuming and heart breaking one.

For we cannot afford to get this done professionally.

But we have also many memories passed down orally…

And so now "The Legend of Mother Luke" is being written, and will be published later.

We offer here a summary of that inspiring and fascinating work.

The Legend of Mother Luke...
.... being the story of Sisters of Grace.

Once upon a time, there was a young girl who loved Jesus more than she loved her life, and longed to serve Him in the poor with all her heart and soul and mind and strength.

When she was only sixteen, she ran away from her rich home, for she was gently and nobly born, to earn her own living, so she could give all she earned to the very poor who thronged the streets.

For she knew that if she stayed where she was, soon she would be married off...

And the Spouse she sought was Jesus Christ.

Had she entered a convent, her contact with the poor would be strictly limited, and that was not what Jesus was asking of her.

She worked in a noisy, dirty factory by day and served the street people after the long hours there.

Soon they knew her goodness and kindness, that she was one of them and kept nothing back for herself.

As years went on, more women sought her out to live with her, and to do the work for Jesus she was doing.

And so the Order was founded.

To own nothing, not a house to live in, not a big convent separating them from the people they served.

Like Jesus, as He teaches in Matthew, they carried nothing for their journey.

Beyond what they needed, they had nothing.

They put on the Holy Habit of Religion. Now everyone saw who they were and knew who they could turn to for sustenance and the lovingkindness of the Lord Jesus.

They lived at first on the streets with those they were supporting. Like Jesus, they had nowhere to lay their heads.

They were not like Nuns from a Convent, who visited the poor then went back to their House.

To earn money to feed the homeless ones, they would gather fruit, anything that would sell, and sit on the street with a barrow.

Earning all they gave and giving all they earned.

Then one day a lady came to them. She knew the work they did and how poorly they lived.

She had been left a small cottage, and God told her in a dream to give them this inheritance.

That little, simple House became a House of Grace; the grace of Jesus providing for his Brides.

There the first Sisters lived, twelve in harmony, and from there Sisters over long years went out, two by two, taking nothing, for they had nothing, to parishes throughout the land, and some overseas.

There too Sisters were formed and trained.

From all classes and walks of life.

All this was 160 years ago, in the south of England.

And as years and decades passed, the way they lived stayed strong and true.

Always reliant on the work of their hands, and on benefactors. On God providing daily for their needs.

For they were not allowed to own property, or to keep money in the bank, even if they had any.

All went to the very poor and hungry.

As it still does.

They never had any "old money" thus; never any coffers to fall back on.

Wherever they lived, they grew food and worked at whatever they could to earn their keep and feed the hungry.

Determined, loving Jesus and living His teachings.

Prayer always their support and strength.

And always, God met their needs.

So they would see an empty house, that was not needed or used, and ask for it.

Not to own it; but simply to use and care for it.

Sometimes a house they rented would be lent to them; to be used by the Order as long as it existed.

Or used for a set time, say five years, after which they would own it and could sell it if they needed to.

Is that a huge thing to ask?

To use a house, a piece of land that is sitting idle?

To live quietly in prayer in a house that no-one needs?

Now these Sisters are in great and urgent need here once more.

Of a quiet place where they can live and use their skills to feed the victims of terrible disasters.

Names like tsunami, Myanmar echo in the heart and will do for many years.

They yearn to do more, but they need here a base, a safe sanctuary.

A refuge where they can live in peace and grow food and emerge from for their work.

They ask nothing more than that, and they would then become invisible – until and unless there is need of their skill and their work.

And then they will respond generously and without stint.

For their original charism stands faithful and true.

It has not changed.

Still dependent on divine providence working through the people of God to reach out in help to the people of God.

Still each and all working every hour they can to feed and clothe Jesus.

Email us on anchoresscj@yahoo.com or graceofchrist@shaw.ca.

Blessings heap upon you…

Tales
from an Irish
Hermitage
by a Nun of Grace

Tales from an Irish Hermitage
Reviews

"Please keep it a secret, but just about everyone on my gift list will receive a copy of this wonderful book for birthdays and other gifting occasions in the coming year.

“You cannot read from this wonderful little book without a smile on your face and happiness in your heart. These stories about animals can teach us much about ourselves and the humans around us. And I happen to know that each story is the absolute truth.

“Where else can you spend so little, receive so much and do so much good, all at once?

“We can hope for many more volumes in the continuing saga of Sister and the critters.”

JA. Texas US

“A few months ago, I was contacted by a nun in Ireland. She was trying to self-publish a book and wondered if I could give her any advice on formatting.

“I already knew her through an online community and had enjoyed her writing very much, so since I had a few weeks of vacation ahead of me, I offered to format the book for her. She sent me the manuscript soon thereafter: *Tales from an Irish Hermitage.*

“This little collection of stories from a tiny hermitage brought me more joy than I anticipated. The author’s style is poetic and flowing, meant to be read aloud. Her tales center around the ragtag animals who come to the hermitage, including an aging ewe named Oonagh, an affectionate gander called Gozzle, and the otherwordly star of ‘Seal Magic.’ The stories bring together the poignancy of life, the beauty of Ireland, and the understated humour of a unique servant of God.

“This is a book for those who love simple, old-fashioned tales. I am privileged to own the first copy that ever came off the presses, for the Sisters asked me to approve the print work before the book was officially released. It has an honoured place on my shelf, where I will reach for it when my heart wants to be soothed or uplifted.

"I encourage you to purchase a copy as well. All of the proceeds from this book go to help care for homeless children in Sri Lanka, where the Sisters are working in the aftermath of tsunami devastation."

RST, Canada

Seasons
of an Irish
Hermitage

by a Nun of Grace

In the “Irish Hermitage” tradition, this book depicts the passing seasons lived by a Nun on an Irish mountain, in reflections, poems and stories. Easter and Christmas hold their true meaning and beauty, amid the exuberance of flora and fauna cherished at the hermitage.

Order from
www.xanga.com/sistersofgraceofchrist
Or email Sisters of Grace at
anchoresscj@yahoo.com or
graceofchrist@shaw.ca

Seasons of an Irish Hermitage
Reviews

"My initial purchase was twelve books to give as gifts to special people. This book affords us a glimpse into a very different way of life from what most of us live. The stories are delightful, and 100% true. The whole family will enjoy Sister's tales."

"It is a 270 page book of stories, poems and reflections, set, like *Tales from an Irish Hermitage*, in the daily life of a Nun living as a Solitary on an Irish mountain.

"Unmistakably Irish - and unmistakably a book of deep Christian faith and life. Those who know the main anchorhold Web site (http://www.iol.ie/~anchorhold) will recognise reflections they enjoyed there....the poems and stories are new, and the book is rich in graphics.

"This beautifully written book follows on from Tales from an Irish Hermitage, with poetry, reflections, stories and observations of the natural world woven into the framework of the passing year.

“No difficult theories, doctrine or dogma here, just the simple truths of day to day Christian living, loving and giving. An inspiration to all seeking a closer walk with Christ, whether they are living in rural Ireland or in the depths of the city.

“Once read, it is a book to be kept on the bedside table to be dipped into at the end of a difficult day.

“All proceeds go to supporting the work of the Sisters caring for the poorest of the poor, in various parts of the world.”

SMG, England

“All the proceeds of sales of this book will go to tend to orphans and the homeless in places around the world. The Nuns can stretch your dollars like you wouldn't believe, but they need the dollars (pounds sterling, euros, etc.).

“This is a charming little book, full of stories, devotions, and prayers. It also gives a fascinating look into a life that most of us can hardly imagine.

"It will make a lovely gift for 'the person who has everything.'"

JA. Texas US

This sequel to *Tales from an Irish Hermitage* brings us back into the life of an Irish nun and the creatures who surround her, told with humour, beauty, and always praise.

LaVergne, TN USA
12 November 2009
163817LV00001B/8/P

9 780980 931730